NEW TESTAMENT
PRAYER
for
EVERYONE

NEW
TESTAMENT
PRAYER
for
EVERYONE

TOM
WRIGHT

First published in Great Britain in 2012

Society for Promoting Christian Knowledge
36 Causton Street
London SW1P 4ST
www.spckpublishing.co.uk

British Library Cataloguing-in-Publication Data
A catalogue record for this book is available from the British Library

ISBN 978–0–281–06906–4
eBook ISBN–978–0–281–06907–1

Typeset by Graphicraft Limited, Hong Kong
First printed in Great Britain by Ashford Colour Press
Subsequently digitally printed in Great Britain

eBook by Graphicraft Limited, Hong Kong

Produced on paper from sustainable forests

CONTENTS

INTRODUCTION

We went into the cathedral for Evensong, and there was the verger looking all round for matches to light the candles. The old matchbox was empty, and someone, it seemed, had taken the spare one that was always kept at the back of the cupboard. Now of course you can still have a service without candles, but in many traditions people value them as a sign of God's mysterious presence. After all, God himself appeared in a pillar of fire to the Israelites in the desert. The symbolism still makes sense.

But what were we to do? None of us were smokers; not a light between us. Then someone noticed, over on the far side of the building, a faint glow coming from one of the side chapels. One of the candles that had been lit for the midday service was still burning. A trail of molten wax had dripped right down to the floor. But the wick was still alight. Just. We lit two new candles from the small flame, and smiled at their comforting, steady light.

We all know we ought to pray, but almost all of us sometimes find it difficult. The matches seem to have been removed, and we can't light the candle. But help is at hand. There, still glowing in a side chapel, are some of the oldest and best prayers ever prayed. They aren't full of long, fancy words. You don't have to be a serious saint to pray them. That's part of the point. The New Testament – where these old prayers are still burning quietly, still sending off a life-giving glow – was written by and for very ordinary people: people who sometimes didn't feel that God was very near them at all; people who wondered how they could even begin to talk to him after the mess they'd made of their lives; people like us.

Prayer, you see, is all about the mysterious reality that our world and God's world are not far apart. Our life and God's life are not separated by a vast distance. (Yes, sometimes we try to put up walls to stop God getting near us, but he can see through them, and sometimes we hear him knocking gently on the other side.) Our sphere of reality and God's sphere of reality – earth and heaven in biblical language – were made to fit together. Prayer is one of the key places where that happens. In fact, some of the biblical prayers, especially the ones in the book of Revelation, seem to be taking place in heaven itself, with us earth-dwellers privileged to eavesdrop at the door.

And of course, at the centre of it all, Jesus himself holds earth and heaven tightly together. That's why his life was so full of both joy and pain: joy at the new creation that was happening all around him; pain because of the darkness that had infected the old creation and was angrily resisting the breaking-in of the new. It is Jesus' own prayers, above all, to which we return again and again: his excited celebration at seeing the power and glory of new creation, his own agony in the garden as he faced the final battle, his solemn and majestic prayer for his followers in the upper room (John 17), and supremely the extraordinary 'Lord's Prayer' he gave to his friends to pray, which they and their successors, including ourselves, have been praying ever since. So as Jesus brought earth and heaven together in his own person, and was himself a man of deep, rich and sometimes agonizing prayer, he invites us to stand at the same spot, which we can do because of his achievement on the cross and his gift of his own spirit. And the way to find our balance, and get our bearings, as we stand there is precisely through prayer.

That is how the New Testament not only tells us to pray and invites us to pray. It draws us into prayer. It helps us to make prayer not just a habit, but the deep heartbeat of our lives. There are four foundational Christian practices that shape us as earth-and-heaven people: prayer, reading the Bible, the sacrament of Holy Communion (or 'Eucharist') and serving the poor. They flow into one another. Jesus led the way and promised to meet us as we do these things. This book brings together two of them, prayer and the Bible, and suggests that one of the important reasons we read the Bible is precisely to get help with our prayers, and that the prayers the Bible itself contains are at the heart of that process.

But prayer isn't just one thing among many. It's like a secret stream, flowing along unseen, refreshing everything else we do and making things happen in ways we can't understand, and often don't even expect, but which prove themselves real time and again. That's why these prayers, these central early Christian prayers going back in some cases to Jesus himself, are worth learning by heart. That way you can slip into them when you're walking along, or waiting for the bus, or peeling potatoes, or drifting off to sleep. They can become the hidden music which sustains our thinking and feeling, music around which we can then learn to improvise, adding harmonies and new rhythms.

The important thing is to start. Prayer is always a journey into the unknown, a voyage of discovery. Sometimes it will feel strange. We will be tempted to give up. But whether we find it hard or easy, the steady flames of prayer from the New Testament will be there so that we can light our own candles from them. They can be the means through which God himself, through his spirit, answers the prayer we pray in that famous hymn:

Come down, O Love Divine;
seek thou this soul of mine . . .
and kindle it, thy holy flame bestowing.

Tom Wright

PART 1

NEW TESTAMENT TEACHING ON PRAYER

1

THE TEACHING OF JESUS

PRAYER IN SECRET
Matthew 6.5–6

> [5]'When you pray, you mustn't be like the play-actors. They love to pray standing in the synagogues and on street corners, so that people will notice them. I'm telling you the truth: they have received their reward in full. [6]No: when you pray, go into your own room, shut the door, and pray to your father who is there in secret. And your father, who sees in secret, will repay you.'

Once, when living in the Middle East, I went out for a walk in the afternoon. On my way home, feeling slightly hungry, I bought a bar of chocolate at a wayside stall. I got back home, went to my room, made a cup of tea, unwrapped the chocolate and broke off a piece to eat it. Fortunately I glanced down at the chocolate before I put it in my mouth. When I did so I dropped it with a shout. It was alive. Inside what looked like a perfectly ordinary bar of chocolate were hundreds of tiny wriggling worms.

Jesus didn't know about chocolate, but he did know about things that looked fine on the outside but were rotten on the inside. Here, at the heart of the Sermon on the Mount, we find his shrewd comments on what it means to live a life that is, so to speak, solid chocolate all the way through.

Jesus doesn't say that outward things don't matter. Giving money to those in need, praying to God day by day, and fasting when it's appropriate – he assumes that people will continue to do all of these. What matters is learning to do them simply to and for God himself. All the Sermon on the Mount, in fact, is centred on God himself, who easily gets squeezed out of religion if we're not careful.

Jesus also assumes that there is benefit to be had from doing these things. Many people imagine that he is asking us to do everything with no thought of reward, and are then rather shocked when he repeats, three times, his belief that our heavenly father will repay us (Matthew 6 verses 4, 6, 18). Clearly, Jesus is not so bothered about the notion of disinterested behaviour, or 'altruism', as we sometimes are. In fact, what he says is far more realistic. If we struggle to clear our hearts of any desire to do something, so that we are acting from totally pure motives, we will always find a little corner of desire somewhere – even the desire to behave altruistically! Then, instead of looking away from ourselves and towards God, we find ourselves focusing back on ourselves again, wanting to please not God but our own ideal of lofty, disinterested action.

The same applies to prayer. What you are in private is what you really are. Go into your inner room and talk to your father. You don't have to make a song and dance about it, and indeed the fewer people that know you're doing it the better. Nor do you have to go on mouthing pious phrases. You may find there are forms of words which help, as a framework or a starting point; Jesus is about to give the disciples the framework he particularly recommends. But the point is to do business with God, one to one.

Jesus doesn't say what kind of reward we should expect. That, too, is part of the point. Simply knowing God better is reward enough; but there may be other things as well. You never know till you try. What is clear is that he is inviting his followers to a life in which inside and outside match perfectly, because both are focused on the God who sees in secret.

THE LORD'S PRAYER

Matthew 6.7–15

[7]"When you pray, don't pile up a jumbled heap of words! That's what the Gentiles do. They reckon that the more they say, the

more likely they are to be heard. [8]So don't be like them. You see, your father knows what you need before you ask him.

[9]'So this is how you should pray:

Our father in heaven,
may your name be honoured
[10]may your kingdom come
may your will be done
as in heaven, so on earth.
[11]Give us today the bread we need now;
[12]and forgive us the things we owe,
as we too have forgiven what was owed to us.
[13]Don't bring us into the great trial,
but rescue us from evil.

[14]'Yes: if you forgive people the wrong they have done, your heavenly father will forgive you as well. [15]But if you don't forgive people, neither will your heavenly father forgive you what you have done wrong.'

I was talking to a friend who had the reputation of being one of the finest preachers in the area. How did he go about it, I asked. He had no particular technique, he said; he just puzzled over the biblical readings that were set for that day until a framework emerged. Once he'd got a framework it was just a matter of writing it out.

That, of course, was a deceptively simple answer, and we can only guess at the hours of struggle and prayer that were disguised by such a short, and humble, response. But it's often the case, in many areas of life, that we blunder around until we find a framework around which we can build. And this is almost always true with prayer.

Jesus contrasts the sort of praying he has in mind with the sort that went on in much of the non-Jewish world. We know from many writings and inscriptions that many non-Jews did indeed use multiple formulae in their prayers: long, complicated magic words which they would repeat over and over in their anxiety to persuade some god or goddess to be favourable to them. Such prayers are often marked by a note of uncertainty. There were many divinities in the ancient pagan world, and nobody quite knew which one might need pacifying next, or with what formula.

This is hardly surprising. Prayer is one of life's great mysteries. Most people pray at least sometimes; some people, in many very different religious traditions, pray a great deal. At its lowest, prayer is shouting into a void on the off-chance there may be someone out there listening. At its highest, prayer merges into love, as the presence of God becomes so real that we pass beyond words and into a sense of his reality, generosity, delight and grace. For most Christians, most of the time, it takes place somewhere in between those two extremes. To be frank, for many people it is not just a mystery but a puzzle. They know they ought to do it but they aren't quite sure how.

What the Lord's Prayer provides, here at the heart of the Sermon on the Mount, is a *framework*. Jesus doesn't say you should always use identical words, and actually when Luke gives his version of the prayer it is different in small but interesting ways (Luke 11.2–4). It looks as though Jesus intended this sequence of thought to act more like the scaffolding than the whole building, though of course the prayer is used as it stands (usually in the longer version we find here in Matthew) by countless Christians every day. Already by Jesus' day the Jewish patterns of prayer were well established, with short but powerful prayers to be said three times a day. Maybe Jesus intended this prayer to be used like that as well.

What then does the prayer tell us about our regular approach to God? First, and so obvious that we might miss it, the prayer is deeply *meaningful*. It isn't a magic formula, an 'abracadabra', which plugs into some secret charm or spell. It is something we can mean with our minds (though it will stretch our thinking) as well as say with our lips. It implies strongly that we humans can and should use our ordinary language in talking to the creator of the universe, and that he wants and intends us to do so. It implies, in other words, that we share with the one true God a world of meaning which he wants us to explore.

Second, everything is set within our calling God 'father' (as Jesus does throughout this Sermon – in fact, we could suggest that a title for the whole Sermon might be, 'What it means to call God "father"'). For Jews in Jesus' day, this title for God went back to God's action in the Exodus, rescuing Israel from Egypt and so demonstrating that 'Israel is my son, my firstborn' (Exodus 4.22).

Third, this God is not a man-made idol. He is the living God, who dwells in 'heaven', and longs to see his sovereign and saving rule come to birth on 'earth'. This is, in fact, a prayer for the kingdom of God to become fully present: not for God's people to be snatched away from earth to heaven, but for the glory and beauty of heaven to be turned into earthly reality as well. When that is done, God's name – his character, his reputation, his very presence – will be held in high honour everywhere. The first half of the prayer is thus all about God. Prayer that doesn't start there is always in danger of concentrating on ourselves, and very soon it stops being prayer altogether and collapses into the random thoughts, fears and longings of our own minds.

Fourth, though, because this God is the creator, who loves his world and his human creatures, we can ask him for everything we need in the safe knowledge that he is far more concerned about it all even than we are ourselves. Much of the rest of the chapter spells this out. But if we are truly praying this prayer to God's honour, we can never simply pray for food for ourselves. We must pray for the needs of the whole world, where millions go hungry and many starve. And already we may sense, bubbling up out of the prayer, the realization that if we truly pray it we might also have to do something about it, to become part of God's answer to our own praying.

Fifth, we pray for forgiveness. Unlike some religions, in which every single action carrys eternal and unbreakable consequences, at the heart of Judaism and Christianity lies the belief that, though human actions matter very deeply, forgiveness is possible and, through God's love, can become actual. Jesus assumes that we will need to ask for forgiveness not on one or two rare occasions but very regularly. This is a sobering thought, but it is matched by the comforting news that forgiveness is freely available as often as we need it.

There is, however, a condition, which remarkably enough is brought right into the prayer itself: we ourselves must be forgiving people. Jesus takes an extra moment afterwards to explain why. The heart that will not open to forgive others will remain closed when God's own forgiveness is offered.

The prayer ends with a sombre and realistic note. Jesus believed that the great time of testing was coming upon the world, and that he would have to walk alone into its darkness. His followers should pray to be spared it. Even now, in the light of Easter and with the guidance and power of the holy spirit, we still need to pray in this way. There will come yet more times of crisis, times when all seems dark for the world, the church, and in our own hearts and lives. If we follow a crucified Messiah, we shouldn't expect to be spared the darkness ourselves. But we must, and may, pray to be kept from its worst ravages, and to be delivered from evil, both in the abstract and in its personified form, 'the evil one'.

Here is the framework Jesus knew we would need. Here is your heavenly father waiting and longing for you to use it day by day as you grow in your knowledge, love and service of him. What is stopping you from making it your own?

ASK, SEARCH, KNOCK
Matthew 7.7–12

⁷'Ask and it will be given to you! Search and you will find! Knock and the door will be opened for you! ⁸Everyone who asks receives;

everyone who searches finds; everyone who knocks will have the door opened. ⁹Don't you see? Supposing your son asks you for bread – which of you is going to give him a stone? ¹⁰Or if he asks for a fish – which of you is going to give him a serpent? ¹¹Well then: if you know how to give good gifts to your children, evil as you are, how much more will your father in heaven give good things to those who ask him!

¹²'So whatever you want people to do to you, do just that to them. Yes; this is what the law and the prophets are all about.'

I hate fundraising. Many people are good at it; many actually enjoy it; but I can't stand it. I hate asking people for things anyway, and asking for money is the worst of all. As a result, I'm not very good at it. I understand that in some countries it's expected that clergy, and people in similar jobs, should cheerfully ask people to give to good causes. In my world, it always seems difficult and embarrassing.

So when I read a passage like this I find it very hard to believe, and I have to remind myself of what it's based on. Does Jesus *really* mean that God is going to answer every request we make? That he is like a father longing to give his children what they want and need? Can we truly take him up on such remarkably open-ended promises?

I think sometimes our failure to believe such promises, and to act on them, doesn't come so much from a failure of faith in God but from a natural human reluctance, like my dislike of fundraising. Maybe I was taught when I was little not to go on asking for things all the time. It's too long ago to remember. But I suspect many people have that instinctive reluctance to ask for things; if pressed, they might say it was selfish, or that God had better things to do with his time than to provide whatever we suddenly happen to want.

Well, that may or may not be true, but it would be a shame to tone down one of the most sparkling and generous sets of promises anywhere in the Bible. Maybe it isn't 'selfish' to ask for things. Maybe it's just the natural thing that children are supposed to do with parents. Maybe our refusal to do so actually makes God sad or puzzled: why aren't his children telling him how it is for them, what they'd like him to do for them? Of course, generosity of spirit is easily abused, and we all know the caricatures of people asking God for wildly inappropriate things in order simply to indulge themselves ('O Lord,' pleads the song, 'Won't you buy me – a Mercedes-Benz?')! The letter of James (4.3) has some stern warnings about asking for the wrong sort of things, and any full discussion of prayer needs to take this into account. But, for most of us, the problem is not that we are too eager to ask for the wrong things. The problem is that we are not nearly eager enough to ask for the right things.

And 'the right things' doesn't simply mean fine moral qualities (though if you dare to pray for holiness, humility or other dangerous things, God may just give them to you). It means the things we need day by day, which God is just as concerned about as we are. If he is a father, let's treat him as a father, not a bureaucrat or dictator who wouldn't want to be bothered with our trivial and irrelevant concerns. It's up to him to decide if he's too busy for us. The fact that there may be a war going on in one country, a famine somewhere else, earthquakes, tragic accidents, murder and pillage all over the place, and that he is grieving over all of them – this might be a problem for a high-ranking authority at the United Nations, but it is no problem whatever for our loving father. When he says he's still got time, space and love to spare for us, we should take him at his word.

Of course, as we become mature children we will increasingly share his concerns for his suffering and sorrowing world. We will want to pray for it more than for ourselves. But, within the kingdom-prayer that Jesus taught us, as well as praying for God's will to be done on earth, we were taught to pray for what we ourselves need here and now. So: what's stopping us?

We may well say that we've tried it and it didn't work. Well, prayer remains a mystery. Sometimes when God seems to answer 'no' we find it puzzling. And people have always found it strange that, if God is supremely wise, powerful and loving, he shouldn't simply do for everybody everything that they could possibly want. Some of the wisest thinkers of today's church have cautiously concluded that, as God's kingdom comes, it isn't God's will to bring it all at once. We couldn't bear it if he did. God is working like an artist with difficult material; *and prayer is the way some of that material co-operates with the artist instead of resisting him.* How that is so we shall never fully understand until we see God face to face. That it is so is one of the most basic Christian insights.

So: treat God as a father, and let him know how things are with you! Ask, search and knock and see what happens! Expect some surprises on the way, but don't expect that God will ever let you down.

PERSISTENCE IN PRAYER

Luke 11.1–13

[1]Once Jesus was praying in a particular place. When he had finished, one of his disciples approached.

'Teach us to pray, Master,' he said, 'just like John taught his disciples.'

[2]'When you pray,' replied Jesus, 'this is what to say:

'Father, may your name be honoured; may your kingdom come; [3]give us each day our daily bread; [4]and forgive us our sins, as we too forgive all our debtors; and don't put us to the test.

[5]'Suppose one of you has a friend,' he said, 'and you go to him in the middle of the night and say, "My dear friend, lend me three loaves of bread! [6]A friend of mine is on a journey and has arrived at my house, and I have nothing to put in front of him!" [7]He will answer from inside his house, "Don't make life difficult for me! The door is already shut, and my children and I are all in bed! I can't get up and give you anything." [8]Let me tell you, even if he can't get up and give you anything just because you're his friend, because of your shameless persistence he will get up and give you whatever you need.

> [9]"So this is my word to you: ask and it will be given you; search and you will find; knock and it will be opened to you. [10]You see, everyone who asks receives! Everyone who searches finds! Everyone who knocks has the door opened for them! [11]If your son asks you for a fish, is there a father among you who will give him a snake? [12]Or if he asks for an egg, will you give him a scorpion? [13]Face it: you are evil. And yet you know how to give good presents to your children. How much more will your heavenly father give the holy spirit to those who ask him!'

The telephone rang. It was a message that my younger son, a singer, was about to get on an aeroplane to go with his choir to the other side of the world. If I was quick, I might just be able to catch him with a call to wish him well. I phoned, caught him, and we had a good chat. There are times when I wonder where fatherhood ends and friendship begins.

Friendship and fatherhood together teach us something about God and prayer. Actually, the learning can be a two-way street. It isn't just a matter of thinking about earthly friends and fathers and then learning that God is like that. There are times when a father needs to take a long, hard look at what God's fatherhood is all about, and start changing his own fatherhood behaviour to be more like it. And most of our friendships, I suspect, could do with the improvement that some reflection about God as a friend might provide.

It is that picture – of God as a friend, in bed and asleep, with his children around him – which probably strikes us as the more peculiar. (We are used to saying that God is our Father, though we may not always ask what exactly that means; but God as our Friend is less obvious.) In the sort of house Jesus has in mind, the family would all sleep side by side on the floor, so that if the father got up at midnight the whole family would be woken up. My children are now past that stage (my wife and I are more likely to be woken up when they come home at midnight or later), but it's obvious what a nuisance it is when the knock comes on the door.

Yet the friend outside has a real problem, and the sleeping friend can and will help him. The laws of hospitality in the ancient Middle East were strict, and if a traveller arrived needing food and shelter one was under an obligation to provide it. The friend in the street knows that the friend in bed will understand; he would do the same if the roles were reversed.

What counts is *persistence*. There are all sorts of ways in which God isn't like a sleepy friend, but Jesus is focusing on one point of comparison only: he is encouraging a kind of holy boldness, a sharp knocking on the door, an insistent asking, a search that refuses to give up. That's what our prayer should be like. This isn't just a routine or formal praying, going through the motions as a daily or weekly task. There is a battle on, a fight with the powers of darkness, and those who have glimpsed the light are called to struggle in prayer – for peace, for reconciliation, for wisdom, for a thousand things for the world and the church, perhaps a hundred or two for one's own family, friends and neighbours, and perhaps a dozen or two for oneself.

There are, of course, too many things to pray about. That's why it's important to be disciplined and regular. If you leave it to the whim of the moment you'll never be a true intercessor, somebody through whose prayers God's love is poured out into the world. But because these things are urgent, important and complex there has to be more to prayer than simply discipline and regularity. Formal prayers, including official liturgies for services in church, are vital for most people for their spiritual health, but they are like the metal shell of a car. To be effective it needs fuel for its engine, and to be effective prayers need energy, too: in this case, the kind of dogged and even funny determination that you'd use with a sleepy friend who you hoped would help you out of a tight spot.

2

THE TEACHING OF PAUL

THE SEARCHER OF HEARTS
Romans 8.22–23, 26–27

²²We know that the entire creation is groaning together, and going through labour pains together, up until the present time. ²³Not only so: we too, we who have the first fruits of the spirit's life within us, are groaning within ourselves, as we eagerly await our adoption, the redemption of our body . . .

²⁶In the same way, too, the spirit comes alongside and helps us in our weakness. We don't know what to pray for as we ought to; but that same spirit pleads on our behalf, with groanings too deep for words. ²⁷And the Searcher of Hearts knows what the spirit is thinking, because the spirit pleads for God's people according to God's will.

How many names can you think of for God? It may sound an odd question. God's proper name in the Old Testament is of course YHWH; but he is referred to in a great many other ways as well, such as 'the Almighty', 'the Holy One of Israel', or 'YHWH of Hosts'. He is, of course, regularly called 'the God of Abraham', sometimes with Isaac and Jacob added as well. Other, stranger names appear fleetingly; Jacob, apparently, knows God as 'the Fear of his father Isaac' (Genesis 31.42, 53) – at least until he wrestles with God face to face in the next chapter.

It would be worth making a study of the various names, titles and descriptions of God scattered liberally around the New Testament as well. In John's gospel, Jesus regularly refers to God in terms of his own mission: 'the father who sent me'. Here in Romans itself, God has been referred to as 'the one who raised Jesus from the dead' (4.24; 8.11). Now, in this passage, we have an equally powerful but more mysterious title: 'the Searcher of Hearts'. This is a disturbing and exciting idea, and we ought to examine it a bit closer.

The word 'searcher' comes from a root which suggests someone lighting a torch and going slowly round a large, dark room full of all sorts of things, looking for something in particular. Or perhaps he is searching in the dark, by listening. What is he wanting to find, and what happens when he finds it?

No doubt God, in searching the dark spaces of our hearts, comes across all sorts of things which we would just as soon remained hidden. But the thing he is wanting to find above all else, and which according to Paul he ought to find in all Christians, is the sound of the spirit's groaning.

Paul's understanding of the spirit is new and striking at this point. At the very moment when we are struggling to pray, and have no idea even what to pray for, just at that point the spirit is most obviously at work. The spirit calls out of us not articulate speech – that would be a relief, and we are not yet ready for relief in this work of prayer – but a groaning which cannot at the moment come into words. This is prayer beyond prayer, diving down into the cold, dark depths beyond human sight or knowing.

But not beyond the Searcher of Hearts. As part of Paul's picture, not just of the world or the church, but of God, we discover that the transcendent creator is continually in communion with the spirit who dwells in the hearts of his people. God understands what the spirit is saying, even though we do not. God hears and answers the prayer which we only know as painful groanings, the tossings and turnings of an unquiet spirit standing before its maker with the pains and puzzles of the world heavy on its heart. There is a challenge here to every church, and every Christian: to be willing to shoulder the task of prayer of this kind, prayer in which we are caught up in the loving, groaning, redeeming dialogue between the father and the spirit.

PRAYING WITH MIND AS WELL AS SPIRIT
1 Corinthians 14.13–19

[13]The one who speaks in a tongue should pray to be able to say the same thing in clear speech. [14]If I pray in a tongue, you see, my spirit prays, but my mind remains fruitless. [15]Why is that important? I will pray with the spirit, and I will pray with the mind as well. I will sing with the spirit, and I will sing with the mind as well. [16]You see, if you say a blessing in the spirit, how can someone who isn't one of the inner circle say the 'Amen' to your prayer? They won't know what you're talking about! [17]You may well be giving thanks in fine style, but the other person isn't being built up. [18]I thank God that I speak in tongues more than all of you. [19]But in the assembly I would rather speak five words with my mind, to teach other people, than a thousand words in a tongue.

When you look at another person, what do you see? I don't mean what shape, what colour, what size of person are you looking at; I mean, how do you think about who they are? How do you observe them as a whole, an entire person and personality?

Some modern traditions, like some ancient ones, have hugely emphasized the importance of the body itself. From fashion models to movie stars, from exercise regimes to slimming programmes, the Western world in particular has given people the message that the most important thing about you is the shape and appearance of your body.

Some other traditions, both ancient and modern, have focused on the mind. Education has sometimes been seen as developing and training the mind, filling it with useful and important information and teaching it how to process it to maximum effect. Those who have not found their education a happy experience have sometimes rebelled against this approach, but focusing on the mind as an almost detachable part of the person is clearly possible.

Other traditions have insisted on the importance of the feelings, the emotions, as the clue to everything. Such an idea often downplays the importance of the mind in favour of things which entrance and delight, which excite and stimulate, which bring a joy or a thrill that doesn't need to be thought about or analysed. Sometimes when people want to talk about this approach they refer to it as the 'heart', knowing quite well that the physical heart itself, the central organ in the body's circulation system, isn't actually where such emotions are located, even though sometimes the physical heart itself does literally beat faster, or experience a sense of warmth or intensity, under strong emotion.

Where in all this do you put the 'spirit'? It's one of the oldest puzzles in Paul that sometimes when he says 'spirit' he is referring to the deepest awareness that a human being is capable of, and sometimes he is referring to God's spirit, the holy spirit.

Rooted as he was in Jewish thinking, Paul saw a human being as a rich, many-sided, complicated but integrated whole. 'Body', 'mind', 'heart', 'soul' and 'spirit' were not, for him, words to describe different *parts* that you could in principle separate out. They were words to describe *the whole person seen from one angle*. In particular, 'spirit' describes the whole person at his or her deepest level of consciousness – which is in fact linked in a thousand ways to mind, heart and body. And 'mind' describes the whole person as a thinking, reasoning being, which is again linked to everything else we are and do.

Paul often has occasion to instruct Christians to let their mind be renewed by God's spirit, as part of their most basic discipleship, living in God's new world. He wants them to think through, and come to know for themselves, what God wants them to do and be (see, for example, Romans 12.1–2). And here he applies this point to worship.

It isn't just that he wants them to engage the mind in order to apply a kind of brake to the unthinking, and hence unchecked, use of spiritual gifts. Nor is it simply – though this is important – that mindless babbling in tongues nobody else can understand is a way of excluding those who don't have a gift like that, or who perhaps are at a very early stage of Christian experience and haven't a clue what's going on (that may be the point he is making in verse 16). These things matter, but there is a bigger issue still.

The underlying point is that Paul wants them to grow to maturity as whole human beings, using and celebrating to the full the various aspects of their created selves, made in God's image. One of the most basic laws of the spiritual life is that you become like what you worship; and if you are worshipping the true God, the creator of all things, the one in whose image you are made, you should be developing as a wise, many-sided human being, not letting one aspect get out of proportion as though God were only interested in the 'spiritual' side, meaning by that not only the non-bodily but also the non-rational. Of course, those who live in a world that has overemphasized the body, or the reasoning mind, may find that they need to redress the balance in other ways than the one Paul stresses here. But the point is this: especially in public worship, what matters is to bring mind, spirit and body together. When you look at a worshipping Christian, what you should see is a whole human being, with every aspect united in giving praise to God.

PRACTICAL PRAYER

Ephesians 6.18–20

[18]Pray on every occasion in the spirit, with every type of prayer and intercession. You'll need to keep awake and alert for this, with all perseverance and intercession for all God's holy ones – [19]and also for me! Please pray that God will give me his words to speak when I open my mouth, so that I can make known, loud and clear, the secret truth of the gospel. [20]That, after all, is why I'm a chained-up ambassador! Pray that I may announce it boldly; that's what I'm duty-bound to do.

Imagine an eagle with clipped wings. Imagine a great ocean-going liner stuck in the Sahara sands. Imagine a basketball player with his ankles tied together. Imagine a railway locomotive in a ploughed field.

Now imagine an ambassador wearing chains in prison. Paul knows it's a bizarre picture, and he puts it like that deliberately to highlight his special need for prayer. An ambassador ought to be free to come and go, to take the message of his king wherever it is needed. How can he do that if they've tied him up?

And yet the eagle is determined to fly, the liner to sail again come what may. He will go on announcing the good news of King Jesus even from a prison cell. Every preacher, everyone who has tried to talk to others about the gospel, will know how he feels as he asks for prayer in his task. How can you find the right words to say? How can you make it clear? How can you get your own mind sufficiently around the extraordinary saving plan of God and then describe it in such a way that other people will find it convincing and compelling?

That's the problem we all face; but for Paul it was worse, granted his situation. And he was determined to do it with full boldness: the word he uses in verse 20 could almost mean 'brazenly'. He is settled in his mind that he will go on talking about King Jesus, his victory over death, and his present and future kingdom, no matter what happens. But he knows that unless people are praying for him he won't be able to do it, and it wouldn't mean anything if he did.

Prayer remains mysterious at one level. Nobody quite knows 'how it works', and this not knowing seems to be part of the point. But it remains a deeply practical thing to do. One of the great Christian leaders of the twentieth century, Archbishop William Temple, declared that whatever else one might say about whether prayer worked, he had noticed that when he prayed, 'coincidences' happened; and when he stopped praying, the 'coincidences' stopped happening. That reminds me of the great golfer who, when someone accused him of being lucky, agreed, but commented that he'd noticed that the more he practised the luckier he got.

Of course, William Temple didn't believe that the things which happened in apparent answer to prayer really were coincidences. This was how God worked. Paul is convinced of the same thing. He knows that the prayers even of young and inexperienced Christians are every bit as powerful and valid in God's presence as those of a seasoned apostle. And he knows that their prayers for him are therefore just as important as his for them.

Prayer is hard work. It can't be reduced to a few moments of sleepy meditation at the end of the day, or a few snatched moments at the beginning. (We must of course add quickly that that would be better than nothing, but only in the same way that a piece of stale bread is better than no food at all, but nowhere near as good as a proper meal.) Paul insists that you'll need to stay awake and keep alert if you're to engage properly in prayer.

If you're going to take praying seriously, you will probably want to plan it out a bit. You may find it helpful to make a few lists of things and people to pray for, not in order to be legalistic or regimented about it but in order to be faithful both to God and to the people who depend upon you for support. Just as in most families there are lists of birthdays, anniversaries and the like, so there is no shame, and plenty of good sense, in keeping a notebook of the people you want to pray for regularly. Some people I know keep a two-sided notebook: the left-hand side to record the prayers they've prayed, the right-hand side to fill in the way in which the prayer was answered (including times when the answer was 'no'). It is remarkable how many small but significant miracles would otherwise be forgotten.

PRAYER FOR THE WORLD

1 Timothy 2.1–7

¹This is my very first command: God's people should make petitions, prayers, intercessions and thanksgivings on behalf of all people – ²on behalf of kings, and all who hold high office, so that we may lead a tranquil and peaceful life, in all godliness and

holiness. ³This is good; it is acceptable with God our saviour, ⁴who wants all people to be saved and to come to know the truth. ⁵For, you see,

> There is one God,
> and also one mediator between God and humans,
> King Jesus, himself a human being.
> ⁶He gave himself as a ransom for all,
> and this was testified when the time was right.

⁷This is why I was appointed a herald and an apostle (I'm speaking the truth, I'm not lying!), a teacher of the Gentiles in faith and truth.

When did you last make a list of people you wanted to pray for? Whose were the first names you wrote down?

Most of us would start with the people we know and love best: our spouse, our children, our parents; other close relatives; friends we see frequently, who are uppermost in our minds; people facing illness or death. Prayer lists often go out in concentric circles, with ourselves in the middle – and we will be sure, no doubt, to pray for all the various concerns that hammer away at us in our own lives, our work, our responsibilities, our worries.

Paul prays for his friends and relatives, of course; we know that from things he says over and over again. But in this passage he strongly urges that we should start, as it were, at the other end. We should pray for the people who hold the world together by their rule, leadership and authority.

For many Christians today, particularly those who (like me) have grown up in the Western world and have never known war or major civil disturbance in our own country, this often seems quite remote. We are happy (more or less) with our democratic institutions, our systems of government. We vote every few years, we answer opinion polls from time to time, and we have a sense that we live in a free society. We're not particularly eager to swap it for another system. Yes, we'd like our politicians to use our tax money more effectively, we grumble about some of their policies, but what they do doesn't drive us to our knees to pray for them, to beseech God to guide them and lead them to create a better world for us all to live in. Many Christians who are reasonably content with their country are tempted to think that praying for kings and governments is a rather boring, conformist thing to do. It looks like propping up the status quo.

But supposing you live (as many readers of this book will do) in countries which have had unstable government, perhaps tyranny, for many years. Supposing you live with the dread of the knock on the door after dark which means that the secret police have come to take someone away, perhaps to be tortured or killed. Supposing 'the government' knows about this, plays along with it, or is even directly responsible. Wouldn't you be praying night and day for good, strong, wise, just rulers who would hold your world together and prevent the bullies and the cynical power-seekers from having it all their own way?

And, since we now live in such a small world, where messages, pictures and sounds can flash around the world in a matter of seconds, where the pain of someone in the Sudan can appear instantly on screens in America or New Zealand, should we not all be joining together and praying for good government on a worldwide scale, for the United Nations and all who seek to influence the rulers of the nations?

This train of thought brings us exactly to the point the Jews had reached in the first century. They had suffered under persecution and unjust rulers for many generations. Pagan monarchs had often tried to squeeze the life out of Judaism. Again and again they had pleaded with God that he would overthrow the oppressive tyrants and give them freedom, as he had done with Pharaoh at the time of the Exodus. But they had also learnt an important lesson about how to conduct themselves while waiting for God's deliverance. When they were in exile in Babylon, and longing for Babylon to be overthrown so they could go home again, the prophet Jeremiah (29.7) told them that during this waiting period they should settle down, live a normal life and *pray to God on behalf of Babylon*. If Babylon was at peace, they would be at peace.

I can just hear some zealous Christians objecting. It's a compromise! Surely we ought to be praying *against* pagan rulers. They exploit their subjects, they oppress people, they are wicked and should be overthrown. Well, in a sense, yes. But God's ways are not our ways, and his timing is not necessarily the timing we would like. Prophets may be called to preach against oppressive regimes. But for ordinary people it is better to be able to go about one's business, to live at peace, to raise a family, to be allowed to worship, without the awful insecurity that comes when governments are unstable or when different regimes follow one another in quick succession.

This was what many Jews of Jesus' day had realized. The Romans made all their subject peoples pray *to* the emperor, invoking him as lord and saviour. But they realized that this wouldn't work with the Jews, who believed that there was only one God; so they allowed them to pray *to* their own God *on behalf of* the emperor. This is the background to the early Christian attitude to praying for those in authority.

And notice how Paul puts it. Pray *for* all those in authority – because this is acceptable to 'God our saviour'! There is only one saviour, and it isn't Caesar, or any other human being, no matter how powerful they are. However surprising it may seem to us, praying for those in authority, even if they are pagan rulers, will become part of God's plan to spread the gospel to all the world. When rulers are doing their job, even if they don't acknowledge God themselves, they create the peace and social stability which will allow God's people to worship without being harassed, and to build up families and communities that follow the way of holiness.

In particular, when the world is at peace, the gospel can spread more easily. God wants people of every race, colour and language to come to him and find the true 'salvation'. Verses 4 and 7 indicate that praying for the peace of the world will be part of the apostolic mission to make this wider salvation a reality.

In the middle of it all, Paul restates his Jewish-style monotheism, to remind his hearers of the basis for this whole approach to prayer for rulers. The rulers are not divine, because there is only one God. Nor can any rulers claim that they are the human embodiment of a divine being, because there is only one person who stands as a 'mediator between God and humans', namely Jesus himself. Verse 5 is rather like 1 Corinthians 8.6: it offers an astonishing redefinition of Jewish monotheism, with Jesus in the middle of it. Like Jewish monotheism, this view of God is what prevents you worshipping earthly rulers, and encourages you instead to pray to God on their behalf. Unlike Jewish monotheism, the fact that this view of God is centred upon Jesus, who died as a ransom for the sins of the whole world (verse 6), means that the news of this one God, this one saviour, must now go out into all the world.

As so often in the New Testament, the call to prayer is also the call to think: to think clearly about God and the world, and God's project for the whole human race. Don't rest content with the simplistic agendas of the world that suggest you should either idolize your present political system or be working to overthrow it. Try praying for your rulers instead, and watch not only what God will do in your society but also how your own attitudes will grow, change and mature.

3

OTHER EARLY CHRISTIAN TEACHING

THE SYMPATHETIC HIGH PRIEST
Hebrews 4.14–16

[14]Since we have a great high priest who has gone right through the heavens, Jesus, God's son, let us hold on firmly to our confession of faith. [15]For we don't have a high priest who is unable to sympathize with our weaknesses, but one who has been tempted in every way just as we are, yet without sin. [16]Let us then come boldly to the throne of grace, so that we may receive mercy, and may find grace to help us at the moment when we need it.

I have just finished reading a fascinating wartime diary, written by an Anglican clergyman who was captured by the Germans in 1940 and spent the next five years in various prison camps, ministering as best he could to the thousands of men who were ill-fed, badly housed and prone to despair. I have learned many things from the book, not least a reminder to be grateful that my own generation, though we have faced many other problems, have at least been spared that kind of experience.

As an appendix to the book, the author included a short essay, a character sketch of an Australian soldier who was in the same camp for a while. Tom Moore was in charge of the Australian barrack, which meant that he was responsible both to the German authorities for the state of the barrack and to the Australians for representing the interests of the men. To quote the writer, John H. King:

> The authorities expect him to see their displeasure when anything is wrong with the state of the barrack or the behaviour of

the men. On the other hand, the men look to him to champion their rights and liberties, real and imagined. To carry out the job efficiently and to retain the confidence of both sides is a rare achievement . . . but Tom succeeded.

He spent most days going to and fro between Germans and Australians, and the other leading figures in the camp, making sure everything was sorted out despite the appalling conditions. He won universal respect.

This is the kind of intermediary role which Hebrews describes in terms of the high priesthood which Jesus continues to hold. Of course, as with some of Jesus' own parables, not all the details fit: I'm not suggesting that God the father is like a hostile officer, or indeed that the church is like an army barrack in a prison camp. But the strong point to which we come is that Jesus has fulfilled the ancient promise of God that he would eventually send his people a great high priest who would do in perpetuity, and perfectly, what the regular priesthood symbolized but could only do in part, and imperfectly.

The promise itself, and the detailed exposition of it, will come shortly. But, by way of introduction, the writer pictures Jesus, like the young Australian officer, as the one who both belongs firmly on 'our side' of the picture and is completely at home, and able to represent us fully and appropriately, on God's side. He was, and remains, one of us, a truly human being who still remembers what it was like to be weak, to get sick, to be tempted over and over from every angle. When he represents us before the father, he isn't looking down on us from a great height and being patronizing about those poor creatures down there who can't really do much for themselves. He can truly sympathize. He has been here. He knows exactly what it's like.

So where is he now, what's he doing and how does it affect us? Verse 14 says that he has 'gone right through the heavens'. Various ancient Jewish writings speak of different levels of 'the heavens'; Paul speaks in 2 Corinthians 12.2 of being caught up into 'the third heaven'. When Solomon built the Temple, he declared that 'heaven and the heaven of heavens cannot contain God' (1 Kings 8.27). Though different writers put it differently, the impression is that within 'heaven' (God's part of the two-sided created order, as opposed to 'earth', the space-time cosmos we humans live in) there are layers, with God's own dwelling being the innermost one.

The point is that Jesus, having died and been raised from the dead, was then exalted, in the ascension, through all the different layers of 'the heavens', right to the very heart, to the throne of the father himself. He didn't, in other words, simply go to a convenient resting place in some spiritual sphere where he could remain, satisfied with having accomplished his earthly work. He went right to his father's inner courtroom, in order that by representing us there, by interceding for us with the father, he might continue to *implement* the work he had *accomplished* on earth. Paul says something similar in Romans 8.34.

So when we come to pray to the heavenly father, we are not shouting across a great gulf. We are not trying to catch the attention of someone who has little or no concern for us. Verse 16 puts it like this: we are coming to 'the throne of grace' (that's a way of saying (a) that we're coming to the throne of God and (b) that we must now think of God as the God of grace), and we may and must come boldly and confidently. This isn't arrogance. Indeed, if we understand who Jesus is, what he's done and what he's still doing on our behalf, the real arrogance would be to refuse to accept his offer of standing before the father on our behalf, to imagine that we had to bypass him and try to do it all ourselves. What is on offer, for those who come to God through Jesus, is 'mercy and grace': mercy, to set us free from the sin and folly in which we would otherwise sink completely; grace, to strengthen us and set us on our feet for our own lives of service and witness.

PRAYING IN FAITH

James 5.13–18

[13]Are any among you suffering? Let them pray. Are any cheerful? Let them sing psalms. [14]Are any among you sick? They should call for the elders of the church, and they should pray over the sick person, anointing them with oil in the name of the Lord. [15]Faithful prayer will rescue the sick person, and the Lord will raise them up. If they have committed any sin, it will be forgiven them. [16]So confess your sins to one another, and pray for one another, that you may be healed.

When a righteous person prays, that prayer carries great power. [17]Elijah was a man with passions like ours, and he prayed and prayed that it might not rain – and it did not rain on the earth for three years and six months. [18]Then he prayed again, the sky gave rain, and the earth produced its fruit.

There are many things in life which look extremely odd to someone who doesn't know what's going on. Imagine watching a craftsman making a musical instrument if you'd never heard music in your life. What, you might think, can such an object possibly be for? Why waste such time and effort on it? Or imagine a child, who has no idea about babies and where they come from, or of the fact that his mother is expecting one soon, watching her get the room ready for the new arrival. It makes no sense. Why this little cot? Why these new decorations?

Of course, when the moment comes all is explained. But sometimes you have to wait; to be patient; to trust that things will come clear. In his letter, James has used other examples, the farmer and the harvest being the obvious one. This theme of patience has run through the whole letter, and marks his thinking out from the ordinary moralism of his day. James is constantly aware of living within a story – living, in fact, within God's story; and of the fact that this story has already reached its climax in his brother Jesus and will one day complete what he had so solidly begun.

This is the setting within which prayer, that most incomprehensible of activities, makes sense. To someone with no idea of God, of there being a world other than what we can touch and see, prayer looks at best like an odd superstition and at worst like serious self-deception. Fancy just talking to yourself and thinking it will make a difference to anything! But almost all human traditions, right across history and culture, have been aware of other dimensions which seem mysteriously to intersect with our own. The ancient Jewish tradition, which comes to fresh and vital expression in Jesus himself and in his early followers and family, sharpens up this general vague awareness of Something Else into not only Someone Else but a named Someone: the God we know in, through and as Jesus himself. Then, suddenly, prayer, and the patience which it involves, make all the sense in the world.

For James to finish his letter with a call to prayer, though perhaps unexpected, is quite appropriate. Prayer must surround everything else that we do, whether sad or happy, suffering or cheerful. The Psalms are there, to this day, as the natural prayer book of Jesus' followers (verse 13), even though many Christians today seem to ignore them altogether. Anointing with oil is there, to this day, as a very simple yet profound and effective sign of God's longing to heal people. Like prayer itself, such an act is mysterious; yet, for those who take what James says seriously, it is full of meaning and power. And forgiveness is there, to this day, as the great open door, the fresh possibility, the chance of a new start, for all who will confess the sin which is dragging them down, and will join in prayer for healing.

James seems, like Jesus himself, to have seen a connection between sin and ill-health. Jesus warned (in John 9) against making too close a link, but at other times, for instance in Mark 2.1–12, it seems that forgiveness and healing went hand in hand. Maybe these are the two things which push to the fore when we take our stand in the place where prayer makes sense, at the place where heaven and earth overlap, and at the place where our own present time and God's future time overlap.

That is, after all, what Christian prayer, and for that matter Christian sacraments, are all about. Prayer isn't just me calling out in the dark to a distant or unknown God. It means what it means and does what it does because God is, as James promised, very near to those who draw near to him. Heaven and earth meet when, in the spirit, someone calls on the name of the Lord. And it means what it means and does what it does because God's new time has broken into the continuing time of this sad old world, so that the person praying stands with one foot in the place of trouble, sickness and sin and with the other foot in the place of healing, forgiveness and hope. Prayer then brings the latter to bear on the former.

To understand all this may require some effort of the imagination. But once you've grasped it, prayer, like that puzzling musical instrument, can begin to play the tune it was designed to play. Suddenly it all makes sense.

That is why James alerts us to the great example of prayer, the archetypal prophet Elijah. There are many lessons one might draw from the story in 1 Kings chapters 17 and 18, but we might not have grasped the point that James is making: that the drought which came as judgment on the people of Israel, and the rain which came when they returned to the Lord and abandoned their idols, all happened in the context of Elijah's prayer. And prayer, of course, is not only a task for the 'professionals', the clergy and Christian leaders. Every Christian has not only the right but the vocation to engage in prayer like that, prayer for one another, prayer for the sick, prayer for the sinners, prayer for the nation and the world. If everyone who reads these words were to determine to devote half an hour every day to this task, the effect could be incalculable.

PART 2

PRAYERS OF THE NEW TESTAMENT

4

PRAYERS OF JESUS

IN THE PRESENCE OF GOD
Matthew 11.25–30

[25]At that time Jesus turned to God with this prayer:

'I give you my praise, father, Lord of heaven and earth! You hid these things from the wise and intelligent and revealed them to children! [26]Yes, father, that's the way you decided to do it! [27]My father gave me everything: nobody knows the son except the father, and nobody knows the father except the son – and anyone the son wants to reveal him to.

[28]'Are you having a real struggle? Come to me! Are you carrying a big load on your back? Come to me – I'll give you a rest! [29]Pick up my yoke and put it on; take lessons from me! My heart is gentle, not arrogant. You'll find the rest you deeply need. [30]My yoke is easy to wear, my load is easy to bear.'

I remember attending a memorial service to honour one of the world's great sportsmen. Colin Cowdrey was one of the greatest cricketers of all time; not quite cricket's Babe Ruth, but not far off. He was known and loved all around the world – not least in India, Australia, Pakistan and the West Indies, whose cricketers had learned to fear and respect his extraordinary ability, and whose crowds had come to love him as a man, not just as a player.

The service was magnificent. Tributes flowed in from around the world; a former prime minister gave the main address; a special song had been written. But for me the most moving moment was when one of Cowdrey's sons came forward and spoke of his father from his inside knowledge. This great public figure, who gave of himself in later life to every good cause he could find, had never lost his close and intimate love for his children and grandchildren. There were many fine stories which only a son could know, and only a son could tell. It was a heart-warming and uplifting occasion.

This remarkable passage in Matthew shows Jesus coming to the same recognition about the one he called 'father'. There were things about his father that, for some reason, only he seemed to know, and only he could tell.

There is a deep mystery here which takes us right to the heart of what it meant to be Jesus. As he announced God's kingdom and put God's powerful love to work in healing, forgiving and bringing new life, he obviously realized that the other people he met, including the religious leaders, his own followers, and the ordinary people, didn't have the same awareness of his father that he did.

Imagine a gifted musician walking around among people who can only just manage to sing in tune. That must have been what it was like for Jesus. He must have known from early on that there was something different about him, that he seemed to have an inside track on knowing who Israel's God truly was, and what he was wanting for his people.

This must have made it all the more galling when he discovered that most of his contemporaries didn't want to hear what he was telling them. Most of them, alarmed at the direct challenge he presented, were either resisting him outright or making excuses for not believing him or following him. Opposition was mounting. And, strangely, this gave Jesus a fresh, further insight into the way his father was operating. This, in turn, resulted in a burst of praise as he glimpsed the strange, unexpected way God was working.

Jewish writings had, for a millennium and more, spoken warmly about the wisdom of the wise. God gave wisdom to those who feared him; a long tradition of Torah-study and piety indicated that those who devoted themselves to learning the law and trying to tease out its finer points would become wise, would ultimately know God. For the average Jew of Jesus' day, this put 'wisdom' about as far out of reach as being a brain surgeon or test pilot seems for most people today. You needed to be a scholar, trained in languages and literature, with leisure to ponder and discuss weighty and complicated matters.

Jesus sliced through all that with a stroke. No, he declared: you just need to be a little child. Jesus had come to know his father the way a son does: not by studying books about him, but by living in his presence, listening for his voice, and learning from him as an apprentice does from a master, by watching and imitating. And he was now discovering that the wise and learned were getting nowhere, and that the 'little people' – the poor, the sinners, the tax-collectors, ordinary folk – were discovering more of God, simply by following him, Jesus, than the learned specialists who declared that what he was doing didn't fit with their complicated theories.

As a result, Jesus had come to see that he was himself acting as a window onto the living God. Where he was, and through his words, people were coming to see who 'the father' really was. He seemed to have the gift and the task of drawing back the curtain and 'unveiling' the truth about God; and the word for 'unveil' here is *apocalypse*, which still today speaks of something dramatic, sudden and earth-shattering.

Wasn't that a bit daunting for his followers? Isn't it rather forbidding to discover that the true God can be known only through Jesus? No. It might have felt like that if it had been somebody else; but with Jesus everything was different. It gave him the platform from which to issue what is still the most welcoming and encouraging invitation ever offered. 'Come to me,' he said, 'and I'll give you rest.' This is the invitation which pulls back the curtain and lets us see who 'the father' really is – and encourages us to come into his loving, welcoming presence.

GLORIFY THE SON

John 17.1–8

[1]After Jesus had said this, he lifted up his eyes to heaven.

'Father,' he said, 'the moment has come. Glorify your son, so that your son may glorify you. [2]Do this in the same way as you did when you gave him authority over all flesh, so that he could give the life of God's coming age to everyone you gave him. ³And by "the life of God's coming age" I mean this: that they should know you, the only true God, and Jesus the Messiah, the one you sent.

⁴'I glorified you on earth, by completing the work you gave me to do. ⁵So now, father, glorify me, alongside yourself, with the glory which I had with you before the world existed.

⁶'I revealed your name to the people you gave me out of the world. They belonged to you; you gave them to me; and they have kept your word. ⁷Now they know that everything which you gave me comes from you. ⁸I have given them the words you gave me, and they have received them. They have come to know, in truth, that I came from you. They have believed that you sent me.'

Shakespeare's play *Hamlet* is full of action. Ghosts, murders, love scenes, plots, accidental killings, betrayals, recriminations and more plots. The play highlights the indecision of the hero when faced with huge problems, and this results in pauses here and there. But at one moment in particular the action comes to a shuddering halt.

Hamlet is looking for an opportunity to take revenge on his stepfather, Claudius, for murdering his father and usurping the throne of Denmark. He comes upon an ideal opportunity: Claudius is in his chamber, kneeling quietly. But Hamlet stops, and thinks. Claudius is praying! If he takes revenge now, Claudius may perhaps have repented and will be saved. Hamlet decides to wait for a better moment. The sorry tale continues.

He is praying! There is a mystery there which nobody can penetrate except the one who is doing the praying. Just as I cannot be sure that when you see something red you are seeing exactly the same colour as I am, so I cannot be sure what passes between you and God when you kneel down and pray. Hamlet couldn't tell what Claudius was praying, but knew he should pause and wait. And, with a totally different king, equally caught up in mystery, intrigue and plots but innocent of all, in John 17 we find ourselves in a place where we, too, should pause and wait, and perhaps quietly join in.

Jesus is praying! Of course, we know that Jesus prayed. The gospels tell us that frequently. But they hardly ever tell us what he prayed or how he prayed. A few sentences at most come down to us, such as that wonderful passage in Matthew (11.25–27), and the burst of praise at the tomb of Lazarus (John 11.41–42). Interestingly, both of those passages look remarkably like shorter versions of what we find in this outstanding, ecstatic chapter. I once heard an actor read the whole of John's gospel, and when he came to chapter 17 he knelt down and prayed it as a prayer. It sounded, and *felt*, like prayer. This is not simply a theological treatise, with John putting ideas together and placing them on Jesus' lips.

Nor, we may suppose, is John remembering it all without having prayed through it himself, over and over again. The mention of 'Jesus the Messiah' in verse 3 sounds very strange from Jesus himself; perhaps here, and maybe elsewhere too, John the praying teacher, in order to make the prayer his own and pass it on to his own followers, has turned phrases round so that they become (so to speak) prayable by the continuing community. But in essence the prayer draws together everything that the gospel story has been about up to this point.

I remember the first time, as a young musician, that I sat in the middle of a school orchestra and played my small part with the music *happening all round me*, instead of coming at me from the loudspeaker of a radio or gramophone. When you make this prayer your own, when you enter into John 17 and see what happens, you are being invited to come into the heart of that intimate relation between Jesus and the father and have it, so to speak, happen all round you. That is both what the prayer embodies and also its central subject matter.

This first section of the prayer is a celebration and a request. The two are closely linked. Jesus is celebrating the fact that his work is done. Yes, there is the huge and awful task awaiting him the next day. But he has completed the deeds and words which the father gave him to do. (Those who see Jesus as simply a great teacher, or think that his task was to heal as many as possible, naturally find this a puzzle.) He has laid before his chosen disciples all that the father has given to him. That is the reason for the celebration, and it is the ground of the request he now makes.

His request is that he may now be exalted, glorified, lifted up to that position alongside the father which in Jewish tradition the king, the Messiah, the son of man, was supposed to attain. The Messiah, say the Psalms, will rule a kingdom that stretches from sea to sea, from 'the River' to 'the ends of the earth' (Psalm 72.8). In other words, he will have a universal dominion. 'One like a son of man' will be exalted to share the throne of God himself (Daniel 7).

When the Messiah takes his seat, exalted over the world, then the age to come will truly have begun – that 'coming age' which Jewish prophets longed for, which Jewish sages taught would appear at the end of 'the present age'. It would be the time of new life, life with a new quality (not just quantity, going on and on for ever). It would be, in our inadequate phrase, 'the life of God's coming age' or 'eternal life'.

This 'eternal life', this life of the coming age, is not just something which people can have after their death. It isn't simply that in some future state the world will go on for ever and ever and we shall be part of it. The point is, rather, that this new sort of life has come to birth in the world in and through Jesus. Once he has completed the final victory over death itself, all his followers, all who trust him and believe that he has truly come from the father, and has truly unveiled the father's character and purpose – all of them can and will possess 'eternal life' right here and now. That, too, is one of the great themes of this gospel (e.g. 3.16; 5.24).

So far, the prayer may seem far too exalted for us to join in. But, as we shall see in the next two sections, the relationship between Jesus and the father, though it seems extraordinarily close and trusting, is not designed to be exclusive. We are invited to join in.

JESUS PRAYS FOR HIS PEOPLE
John 17.9–19

[9]'I'm praying for them. I'm not praying for the world, but for the people you've given me. They belong to you. [10]All mine are yours; all yours are mine; and I'm glorified in them.

[11]'I'm not in the world any longer, but they're still in the world; I'm coming to you. Holy father, keep them in your name, the name you've given to me, so that they may be one, just as we are one.

[12]'When I was with them, I kept them in your name, the name you've given me. I guarded them, and none of them has been destroyed (except the son of destruction; that's what the Bible said would happen). [13]But now I'm coming to you. I'm speaking these things in the world, so that they can have my joy fulfilled in them.

[14]'I have given them your word. The world hated them, because they are not from the world, just as I am not from the world. [15]I'm not asking that you should take them out of the world, but that you should keep them from the evil one. [16]They didn't come from the world, just as I didn't come from the world. [17]Set them apart for yourself in the truth; your word is truth. [18]Just as you sent me into the world, so I sent them into the world. [19]And on their account I set myself apart for you, so that they, too, may be set apart for you in the truth.'

In the newspapers some time ago, I read that a mother had been punished by the courts. She had left her two young children entirely by themselves, while she went off for a foreign holiday with her new boyfriend. (The father, it seems, was nowhere to be found.) It is hard to believe that a mother could do such a thing. One wonders what she thought she would find when she got home. Tragically, such things happen in our world today.

But supposing she herself had had loving parents who were only too glad to look after the children while she was away? That would have made all the difference. She could have entrusted the little ones to them, safe in the knowledge that they would care for them as much as she did. One can imagine a mother in that situation giving her parents detailed instructions as to how each child should be looked after, not because she didn't trust her parents to look after them but because she did.

What Jesus prays here grows out of the fact that he is going away. He is entrusting the disciples to the father he has known and loved throughout his own earthly life, the father who, he knows, will care for them every bit as much as he has done himself. He is very much aware that the disciples are at risk. The world, which hates them as it hated him, will threaten and abuse them. They don't belong to it, but they are to be sent into it, and they need protecting. That's what the prayer is about.

This passage begins with a description of who Jesus' followers are. They are the ones the father has given to Jesus; they already belong to him, and Jesus is handing them back into his safe keeping. They are distinct from 'the world'. Insofar as they are the new, cleansed people they have become through Jesus' call and teaching (see John 15.3), they are not 'from the world'.

This can seem puzzling, and we'd better explain it a bit more. Jesus is not suggesting that his followers don't possess human ancestry, homes and families, and physical bodies which will one day decay and die. 'The world' in this gospel doesn't mean simply the physical universe as we know it. It means the world insofar as it has rebelled against God, has chosen darkness rather than light, and has organized itself to oppose the creator. Seen from within that 'world', Jesus is 'from' elsewhere. So too, we discover to our surprise, are the disciples. In other words, 'the world' in this dark sense is not the place, the force, the sphere, that determines who the disciples most truly are.

What they now need, therefore, is to be kept from being pulled back into 'the world' with all its wickedness and rebellion. During his public ministry, teaching them and leading them, Jesus has looked after them, like the shepherd with his sheep. Now, because he is coming to the father, he is entrusting them to the father, who will continue the work of keeping them safe.

He therefore addresses the father as 'holy' (verse 11), and declares that he is 'setting himself apart' so that the disciples too may be 'set apart'. The word for 'setting apart' is basically the same as the word for 'holy'; but our word 'holy', when applied to people, can give a sense of over-pious religiosity which is foreign to the New Testament. What is 'holiness' in Jesus' world?

In first-century Judaism, 'holiness' called to mind the Temple in particular. It was the holy place, the place where the holy God had promised to live. It referred particularly to the Holy of Holies, the innermost shrine, where the high priest would go once a year to make atonement for the people. The high priest had to go through special ceremonies of 'consecration', to be 'set apart' so that he could enter into the presence of the holy God, and pray there for his people. In exactly the same way, Jesus is declaring that he has been, all along, 'set apart', 'consecrated' for God's exclusive service. Now, like the high priest, he is asking the father to preserve his people from evil, from the tricks and traps of 'the world'. He wants them to be his holy people in the best and fullest sense.

What Jesus has already done for them is to 'keep' them in the father's name (verse 12) and to give them his word (verse 14). In other words, when he now entrusts them to the father, this won't mean a sudden change, like a mother entrusting her children to someone of whom they've never heard and whose house will be run on quite different lines to their own home. He has already taught them, so to speak, the table manners appropriate for the father's house. In praying for them now, he is simply praying that what he has begun, the father will gloriously complete.

This prayer has been used for many centuries by pastors, teachers and other Christian leaders as they pray for those in their care. It can also, with only slight variation, be used by Christians of all sorts for themselves. Substitute 'Jesus' where the prayer says 'I', and replace 'they' and 'them' with 'I' and 'me', and you'll get the idea. But be careful. This is a serious prayer. It is one of the most serious things Jesus ever said. That's why, deep down, it is also among the most joyful and hopeful. Pray it with awe, and with delight.

THAT THEY MAY BE ONE
John 17.20–26

²⁰'I'm not simply praying for them. I'm praying, too, for the people who will come to believe in me because of their word. ²¹I am praying that they may all be one – just as you, father, are in me, and I in you, that they too may be in us, so that the world may believe that you sent me.

²²'I have given them the glory which you have given to me, so that they may be one, just as we are one. ²³I in them, and you in me; yes, they must be completely one, so that the world may know that you sent me, and that you loved them just as you loved me.

²⁴'Father, I want the ones you've given me to be with me where I am. I want them to see my glory, the glory which you've given me, because you loved me before the foundation of the world.

²⁵'Righteous father, even the world didn't know you. But I have known you, and these ones have known that you sent me. ²⁶I made your name known to them – yes, and I will make it known; so that the love with which you loved me may be in them, and I in them.'

This afternoon I looked on the Internet for a website about an electric appliance that's gone wrong. I've lost the instruction booklet and was hoping to find relevant information through the Web.

I found the website of the company that makes the appliance and looked for information about it. I then spotted that there was a special category entitled 'Frequently Asked Questions'. FAQs for short. Exactly what I needed . . .

In the church where I work, people come from all over the world. Many of them have never been in an Anglican (Episcopal) church before. Our most frequently asked question comes because they are puzzled by what we say every day during worship, in the words of one of the creeds (the great statements of belief produced by the early Christians). What puzzles them is when we say that we believe in the 'one, holy, catholic and apostolic church'. Surely, they say on the way out, you are Anglicans, not Catholics? Why do you say you believe in the 'catholic' church?

The answer is that the word 'catholic' simply means 'universal'. Of course, many people say 'catholic' when what they strictly mean is 'Roman Catholic'. That's where the confusion arises. But, since many people, including many practising Christians, don't often think about what the church actually is, and why, this gives an opportunity to say something more. And this section, the end of Jesus' great prayer, is where a good deal of our view of the church comes from.

Imagine some great figure of the past. Shakespeare, perhaps. George Washington, possibly. Socrates. Think of someone you respect and admire. Now imagine that the historians have just found, among old manuscripts, a letter from the great man himself. And imagine that it was talking about . . . you. How would you feel?

That is how you should feel as you read verse 20. Jesus is talking about *you*. And me. 'Those who believe in me through their word', that is, through the word of his followers. His followers announced the message around the world. Those who heard them passed it on. And on, and on, and on. The church is never more than one generation away from extinction; all it would take is for a single generation not to hand the word on. But it's never happened. People have always told other people. I am writing this book, and you are reading it, as a result. It's awesome, when you come to think about it.

But what is Jesus praying for, as he thinks about you and me and all his other followers in this and every generation? He is praying that we may be, just as the old words say, 'one, holy and universal,' founded on the teaching of the followers, the 'apostles', the ones who were with him on that occasion. In particular, he longed that we should all be one. United.

This unity isn't to be just a formal arrangement. It isn't just an outward thing. It is based on, and must mirror, nothing less than the unity between the father and the son. Just as the father is in the son, and the son in the father, so we too are to live within that unity. That can only mean that we ourselves are to be united. And, in case we might miss the point, the result of this will be that the world will see, and know, that this kind of human community, united across all traditional barriers of race, custom, gender or class, can only come from the action of the creator God. 'So that the world may believe . . .'

This picks up what Jesus has said earlier, in John 13.35. 'This is how all people will know that you are my disciples: if you have love for each other.' Unity is vital. Often we sense it, heard like soft music through the partition walls we set up around ourselves. Sometimes we experience it, when for a moment we meet Christians from a totally different background and discover that, despite our many differences, and the traditions that keep us apart, we know a unity of love and devotion that cannot be broken. But just as often, alas, we experience, sense and know that Jesus' prayer for us has not yet been fully answered.

As in any human relationship, unity cannot be forced. There can be no bullying, no manipulation. But in a divided world, where the divisions have often run down so-called 'religious' lines, there is no excuse for Christians not to work afresh in every generation towards the unity Jesus prayed for. If we are, essentially, one in faith, there can be no final reason why we may not be one, also, in our life and worship.

In addition, Jesus returns to another, earlier theme (see John 12.26 and 14.3). His followers are to be 'with him', to see his glory. They are to know and experience the fact that the father has exalted him as the sovereign of the world. They are to know that the love which the creator God has given to him has installed him as the loving Lord of all.

Many Christians today draw back from that statement. They suppose, naturally enough, that it will sound arrogant, or as though they are giving themselves a special status by claiming this about Jesus. But this is to misunderstand the whole message of the gospel. When Jesus is exalted, the reason is nothing other than love. This is not the sort of sovereignty that enables people to think themselves better than others. It is the sort of sovereignty that commits them, as it committed Jesus, to loving service.

That's what the whole prayer comes down to in the end (verse 26). It is about the love of the father surrounding Jesus, and this same love, as a bond and badge, surrounding all Jesus' people, making him present to them and through them to the world. In verse 11 Jesus addressed the father as 'holy'; now he addresses him as 'righteous' (verse 25). The father is the judge of all the earth; though the world rages against Jesus' followers, he will see that right will prevail.

But, as always in the New Testament, the justice for which we pray, the righteous judgment through which the father expresses himself in his world, appears before us as love. That is because, supremely, it appears before us in the person of Jesus: this Jesus, this man who prayed for you and me, this high priest who set himself apart for the father's glad service.

GETHSEMANE

Matthew 26.36–46

[36]So Jesus went with them to the place called Gethsemane.

'You sit here,' he said to the disciples, 'while I go over there and pray.'

[37]He took Peter and the two sons of Zebedee with him, and began to be very upset and distressed.

[38]'My soul is overwhelmed with grief,' he said, 'even to death. Stay here and keep watch with me.'

[39]Then, going a little further on, he fell on his face and prayed.

'My father,' he said, 'if it's possible – please, please let this cup go away from me! But . . . not what I want, but what you want.'

[40]He came back to the disciples and found them asleep.

'So,' he said to Peter, 'couldn't you keep watch with me for a single hour? [41]Watch and pray so that you don't get pulled down into the time of testing. The spirit is eager, but the body is weak.'

[42]Again, for the second time, he went off and said, 'My father, if it's not possible for this to pass unless I drink it, let your will be done.'

[43] Again he came and found them asleep; their eyes were heavy. [44] Once more he left them and went away. He prayed for the third time, using the same words once again. [45] Then he came back to the disciples.

'You can sleep now,' he said, 'and have a good rest! Look – the time has come, and the son of man is given over into the hands of wicked people! [46] Get up and let's be going. Look! Here comes the one who's going to betray me!'

There was once a small girl who had never seen her father anything but cheerful.

As long as she could remember, he seemed to have been smiling at her. He had smiled when she was born, the daughter he had longed for. He had smiled as he held her in his arms and helped her to learn to eat and drink. He had laughed as he played with her, encouraged her with games and toys as she learned to walk, chatted brightly as he took her to school. If she hurt herself, his smile and gentle kiss helped her to relax and get over it. If she was in difficulties or trouble, the shadow that would cross his face was like a small cloud which hardly succeeded in hiding the sun; soon the smile would come out again, the eager interest in some new project, something to distract, to move on to new worlds.

And then one day it happened.

To begin with she wasn't told why. He came back home from a visit, and with a look she'd never seen before went straight to his room. Ever afterwards she would remember the sounds she then heard, the sounds she never thought to hear.

The sound of a healthy, strapping 30-year-old man weeping for a dead sister.

It was of course a necessary part of growing up. In most families, grief would have struck sooner. Looking back, she remained grateful for the years when smiles and laughter were all she could remember. But the shock of his sudden vulnerability, far more than the fact of the death of her aunt and all that it meant, were what made the deepest impression.

I think Gethsemane was the equivalent moment for the disciples.

Oh, Jesus had been sad at various times. He'd been frustrated with them for not understanding what he was talking about. He'd been cross with the people who were attacking him, misunderstanding him, accusing him of all sorts of ridiculous things. There had even been tension with his own family. But basically he'd always been the strong one. Always ready with another story, another sharp one-liner to turn the tables on some probing questioner, another soaring vision of God and the kingdom. It was always they who had the problems, he who had the answers.

And now this.

Jesus was like a man in a waking nightmare. He could see, as though it was before his very eyes, the cup. Not the cup he had spoken of, and given them to drink, in the intense atmosphere of the Last Supper an hour or so before. This was the cup he had mentioned to James and John (in Matthew 20.22–23), the cup the prophets had spoken of. The cup of God's wrath.

He didn't want to drink it. He badly didn't want to. Jesus at this point was no hero-figure, marching boldly towards his oncoming fate. He was no Socrates, drinking the poison and telling his friends to stop crying because he was going to a much better life. He was a man, as we might say, in melt-down mode. He had looked into the darkness and seen the grinning faces of all the demons in the world looking back at him. And he begged and begged his father not to bring him to the point of going through with it. He prayed the prayer he had taught them to pray: Don't let us be brought into the time of testing, the time of deepest trial!

And the answer was No.

Actually, we can see the answer being given, more subtly than that implies, as the first frantic and panicky prayer turns into the second and then the third. To begin with, a straight request ('Let the cup pass me by'), with a sad recognition that God has the right to say 'No' if that's the way it has to be. Then, a prayer which echoes another phrase in the Lord's Prayer: if it has to be, 'may your will be done'. The disciples probably didn't realize that, when Jesus gave them the Lord's Prayer (Matthew 6.9–13), this much of it would be so directly relevant to him. He had to live what he taught. Indeed, the whole Sermon on the Mount seemed to be coming true in him, as he himself faced the suffering and sorrow of which he'd spoken, on his way to being struck on the cheek, to being cursed and responding with blessings. Here, for the second time in Matthew's narrative (the first time being the temptation story in 4.1–11), we see Jesus fighting in private the spiritual battle he needed to win if he was then to stand in public and speak, and live, and die for God's kingdom.

The shocking lesson for the disciples can, of course, be turned to excellent use if we learn, in our own prayer, to wait with them, to keep awake and watch with Jesus. At any given moment, someone we know is facing darkness and horror: illness, death, bereavement, torture, catastrophe, loss. They ask us, perhaps silently, to stay with them, to watch and pray alongside them.

Distance is no object. In any one day we may be called to kneel in Gethsemane beside someone dying in a hospital in Nairobi, someone being tortured for their faith in Burma, someone who has lost a job in New York, someone else waiting anxiously for a doctor's report in Edinburgh. Once we ourselves get over the shock of realizing that all our friends, neighbours and family, and even the people we have come to rely on, are themselves vulnerable and need our support – if even Jesus longed for his friends' support, how much more should we! – we should be prepared to give it to the fullest of our ability.

And when we ourselves find the ground giving way beneath our feet, as sooner or later we shall, Gethsemane is where to go. That is where we find that the Lord of the world, the one to whom is now committed all authority (Matthew 28.18), has been there before us.

5

PRAYERS OF PAUL

TO GOD BE THE GLORY

Romans 11.33–36

> [33]O, the depth of the riches
> and the wisdom and knowledge of God!
> We cannot search his judgments,
> we cannot fathom his ways.
> [34]For 'who has known the mind of the Lord?
> Or who has given him counsel?
> [35]Who has given a gift to him
> which needs to be repaid?'
> [36]For from him, through him and to him are all things.
> Glory to him for ever! Amen.

I was taken yesterday to see the site of a new bridge across
a river.

We parked the car in a grassy wood and set off to walk. The
trees were quite thick to begin with, and I couldn't see the river,
though I could hear it. I assumed the bridge was to be an ordinary
one, connecting two banks not far apart, at a height of maybe
fifteen or twenty feet above the water.

Suddenly, as the trees thinned out, I looked from side to side
and realized to my alarm that we were on a ledge jutting out
with sheer sides and a long drop. There was a wall ahead of us,
preventing us seeing where we were going. We carefully squeezed
round the edge of the wall and found ourselves on a ledge, looking
down a hundred feet and more to the swirling river below. This
was where an old railway bridge had crossed the river, thirty
years ago, on a huge viaduct. Only the stone pillars at either side
remained. The plan, so my guides explained, was to reconnect

the two sides with a suspension footbridge. It would be spectacular, breathtaking.

I couldn't go too near the edge. I am all right with heights up to a point, but there was no fence, and a strong wind was blowing. I was filled with admiration for the daring, the simplicity and the skill both of the plan and of how the finished product would look.

That is how Paul expects us to feel as we come round the last bend in this, the greatest of his letters. We may not have expected to emerge at this point with this view. We are certainly liable to find ourselves suffering from theological vertigo, if not sheer terror, as well as intellectual exhaustion. But there is a wonderful simplicity about the argument, or rather about the plan of God as Paul has laid it out. It looks dangerous, and indeed, in one sense, it is; it is always possible for people to take this bit or that bit of what he says and construct a scheme of their own which doesn't quite manage to keep its balance the way Paul has done. No doubt some may think my own treatment is guilty of this too, and that may well be the case. But this is the point in the argument when the only thing left to do is to take a long, deep breath and shake our heads in wonderment, and give praise to the God whose thoughts, plans and accomplishments are so much deeper and greater than anything we could have imagined for ourselves.

When Jewish people want to praise God, they have a rich tradition to draw on in the Bible, and Paul draws together several passages to heap up not only praise itself but the echoes of Israel's praise down the ages. The Psalms are full of declarations of how extraordinary God is in his wisdom and love. Proverbs and Job celebrate that sense of wonder and mystery at the way in which God is always out ahead of us, ready to surprise us by doing new things which none the less, in retrospect, are exactly right and full of rich wisdom and insight far beyond anything we could have fathomed. Passages like Job 5.9, 15.8 and 36.22 and 23 echo underneath verses 33 and 34; verse 35 then quotes directly from Job 41.11, near the conclusion of that great book. God is never in anyone's debt. It is a perpetual human failing to imagine that he is – to suppose that we can establish a claim on God either by our birth, our beauty, our brains or our behaviour. But we can't. Nobody is ever in the position of giving God a gift which demands repayment while they sit back smugly, knowing they are in the right and waiting for God to get his act together.

In fact, as the final verse indicates in a triumphant sweep of thought, everything we are comes from him. Everything we have comes from him. Everything that exists, the whole of creation, is his handiwork and is sustained in existence by his power and love. Everything we do traces itself back into his presence as the sovereign one before whom all human work and activity is, at best, loving service.

The project of God's new creation, like the proposed bridge over the river we were imagining, is not yet complete. But the architect has designed it. The foundations are securely laid. The work is already well in hand. The final completion is not in doubt. It is time to stand back, not exactly in admiration – that implies a kind of cool appraisal, an approving nod from one who might in principle have done such a thing themselves – but in sheer awe and breathtaking wonder at the scale and scope of it all. Glory to God for ever! Amen.

TO THE ONLY WISE GOD

Romans 16.25–27

[25]Now to him who is able to strengthen you according to my gospel, the proclamation of Jesus the Messiah, in accordance with the unveiling of the mystery kept hidden for long ages [26]but now revealed and made known through the prophetic writings, according to the command of the eternal God, for the obedience of faith among all the nations – [27]to the only wise God, through Jesus the Messiah, to whom be glory to the coming ages! Amen.

I watched as the children played in the swimming pool. The water was about four feet deep. Three of them stood side by side, with linked arms. Then they squatted down, with only their noses above water, and two others climbed on to their shoulders. Then a younger boy scrambled up on to *their* shoulders. Then, slowly but surely, the three at the bottom stood up, until the whole pyramid was nearly, very nearly, standing proudly upright.

At that moment two other children, seeing the fun, came to join in. Despite shouts of warning from some of those already involved, they tried to get in on the act, scrabbling and clutching and trying to join the little one up on the top. The whole pyramid began to wobble, and suddenly they all toppled over with legs and arms going in every direction and the most enormous splash I had ever seen in the pool.

That is, more or less, what has happened with the last sentence of this great letter. I think, actually, that Paul probably intended it this way. If he didn't – if, in other words, it just came out like that in his dictation and he didn't bother to correct it – I think he was happy with it, happy to make a final splash even though the construction of the sentence eventually gets top-heavy and falls over with legs and arms (extra phrases and clauses tagged in here and there) all over the place. Let's look at it and see how the pyramid was at least designed to work before the extra bits were added.

The bottom row of the pyramid is meant to say: 'To God be the glory for ever!' This divides up into three sections, closely linked. First, God is described in terms of what he can do for the Christians in Rome (for all Christians, of course, but Paul wants this church to know this in particular): he can give them strength through the gospel. Second, what has happened in the gospel is the fulfilment of the age-old story of God, Israel and the world. Third, this gospel has been spread around the world to bring about the obedience of faith. So far, so good.

Standing on the shoulders of these basic points are two more. First, the gospel has been made known through the prophetic writings: Paul may have in mind the Old Testament scriptures, or he may even be referring to some early Christian texts. Second, this has come about because of the command of God, the eternal one. Paul is clearly heaping up phrases which echo, or refer back to, entire sections of the letter that is now drawing rapidly to its close. So much of what he has been writing about has been to do with the way in which the long narrative of Israel has come to fulfilment and fruition in Jesus the Messiah, and with the way in which God himself, at work in and through Jesus, is now still at work through the announcement of the gospel.

What Paul then puts on top of the pyramid looks as though it's going to be: 'To the only wise God be glory for ever.' But then, like the extra child at the last minute, he realizes that he can hardly bring this letter of all letters to a conclusion without Jesus being in the very middle of it. So he adds one more phrase, which makes the whole sentence fall over, grammatically speaking, with a great splash: 'To the only wise God . . . *through Jesus the Messiah* . . . to whom be glory to the coming ages!'

Was the glory going to God, or to Jesus? Does it matter? Paul would certainly have said, 'No, it doesn't'. Jesus is both Israel's Messiah according to the flesh and also 'God over all, blessed for ever'. Paul takes Old Testament passages which clearly refer to 'the Lord', meaning YHWH, the God of Israel, and transfers them so that they now refer to Jesus. What theologians call a 'high Christology' – a view of Jesus which sees him as fully and completely divine as well as fully and completely human – doesn't have to wait for later centuries and writers. It is already fully present in Paul.

In particular, we note that Paul refers in the closing phrases to God as 'the only wise God'. There were many other claims to wisdom in the ancient world. There were many other gods who offered insight, of a sort and at a cost. There were plenty of teachings about how to live, how to think, what to believe, how to pray. But Paul believes – and the powerful gospel of Jesus bears him out – that there is only one God who is truly wise. He is the creator. He understands how the whole world works, what humans are and how they think, where they go wrong and how they can be put to rights, and how, when that happens, the whole of creation will dance for joy at its new-found freedom. This is the hidden wisdom which formed the secret plan, the plan now unveiled in the gospel, the gospel which now evokes as its proper response 'the obedience of faith' (as in Romans 1.5), the faith which is open to the whole world. When you see the end from the beginning in this way; when you glimpse even a little of what Paul has glimpsed of the wisdom, love, grace, power and glory of the eternal God revealed in Jesus the Messiah – then you, too, will want to join him in piling up all the glory and praise and love and adoration you can muster. And you won't care how big a splash you make as you do so.

GRACE, LOVE AND FELLOWSHIP
2 Corinthians 13.13

[13]The grace of King Jesus the Lord, the love of God, and the fellowship of the holy spirit be with you all.

The final sentence of 2 Corinthians is one of the most famous lines anywhere in Paul – so famous, in fact, that many people who hear it, or say it regularly, don't even realize it *is* by Paul, and wouldn't be able to find it if they thought it was. It's become a regular prayer, or blessing, in many churches and Christian groups. It sums up so much of what being a Christian is all about; it draws the focus firmly on to the God we know in and through Jesus and the spirit; and it takes the rich practical meaning and the rich theological meaning and turns them together into an elegant prayer. No wonder it has become so popular.

It's worth pausing on this verse and digging a little deeper, before we let the familiar words wash over us and forget what they actually mean. Let's begin with what they say about being a Christian.

Being a Christian starts with *grace*. The reason we are what we are is because the living God has reached down to us in sheer undeserved mercy. That's what Paul celebrates repeatedly in his gospel. But Paul can also use the word 'grace' to describe not only what God freely and lovingly does *for* us, but also what he does *in* us and *through* us; more particularly, to describe what God did in and through the churches in Macedonia when he stirred them up to give generously, even beyond their means. There is solid sense to this second meaning, because 'grace' principally referred to the totally generous and self-giving love of God. We shouldn't be surprised if those whose lives are transformed by grace become generous and self-giving people.

So why does Paul speak of the grace of *Jesus*, the King, the Lord, rather than simply of God? Well, he has spoken about it previously: in chapter 8 verse 9 he urged the Corinthians to give generously, using the example of Jesus himself, leaving the riches of his heavenly existence and choosing to become poor and humble on our behalf. We could put it like this: Jesus is the person the generous and self-giving God became. Jesus *embodied* the grace of God. In Jesus grace became human, because that's what grace needed to do to be fully itself, to give itself for the world. We can properly speak, therefore, of 'the grace of the Lord, King Jesus', and we can pray, as Paul does here, that this grace will be powerfully active in the life of the church. That sums up one entire train of thought in this letter.

But behind and around this specific active power is 'the love of God'. In the New Testament, God's love is not simply one aspect of his character; it is the very heart, the essence of who God is. Love is, of course, a deeply personal quality, perhaps we should say the highest personal quality there is. And it is noticeable that the Jewish and Christian declaration of belief in a God of love as the only true God stands out a mile from most other views of God ancient or modern. The ancient pagan world certainly didn't believe in a God of love. Some of the gods and goddesses might show love, of a kind, for certain people, but that world was full of the anxiety that comes from a fear of superhuman forces that are precisely not loving, but are instead capricious, malevolent, and needing to be pacified or placated. None of the multiple options in that most pluralist of religious worlds spoke of a single God whose innermost nature was love.

This is hardly surprising, because the experience of life that most people have is hardly one of unmixed happiness; and, if there is one God who made the world, most people who think at all about the world will conclude that this God can hardly be loving. But what Judaism clung to as hope, and what Christianity announced as fulfilled at last, was the belief that the one God who made the world *was* indeed a totally loving God, who would demonstrate this love by acting within the world, at enormous cost to himself, to put everything right at last. And in gazing upon that loving God, and learning to trust and love him in return, the early Christians found themselves embraced in a new kind of spirituality, an intimacy of trust like that of children with a father, a warm security of knowing that they were loved with an everlasting love. That is what Paul means by 'the love of God'.

But those who are grasped by this love, who have the grace of the Lord Jesus in their bloodstreams, are thereby joined together in a family which the world has never seen before. It is a family not at all based on physical or ethnic descent or relation; anyone and everyone is welcome in it, which was just as challenging to most ancient people as it is to most modern ones. It is a family called to share a common life, and the word Paul uses here, *koinonia*, can be translated 'partnership', 'association', 'participation', 'sharing', 'communion', or even 'interchange', as well as the familiar 'fellowship'. This *koinonia* has been under enormous strain as Paul and the Corinthians have struggled to work out their relationship through visits, letters, reports, rumours, sorrow, joy, despair and hope. It is because Paul believes passionately that God's own spirit is at work in both his life and that of the Corinthians that he cannot let them go, cannot walk away and found another church somewhere else, cannot simply bask in the happy relationship he enjoys with his beloved Macedonian churches, but must thrash things out, must let partnership, participation and fellowship have their full expression. Indeed, if you want to know what 'the fellowship of the holy spirit' means in practice, a slow and serious reading of 2 Corinthians is a good, if sobering, place to start.

BLESSINGS ON THE SOVEREIGN GOD!
Ephesians 1.3–10

[3]Let us bless God, the father of our Lord Jesus, the king! He has blessed us in the king with every spirit-inspired blessing in the heavenly realm. [4]He chose us in him before the world was made, so as to be holy and irreproachable before him in love. [5]He fore-ordained us for himself, to be adopted as sons and daughters through Jesus the king. That's how he wanted it, and that's what gave him delight, [6]so that the glory of his grace, the grace he poured on us in his beloved one, might receive its due praise.

[7]In the king, and through his blood, we have deliverance – that is, our sins have been forgiven – through the wealth of his grace [8]which he lavished on us. Yes, with all wisdom and insight [9]he has made known to us the secret of his purpose, just as he wanted it to be and set it forward in him [10]as a blueprint for when the time was ripe. His plan was to sum up the whole cosmos in the king – yes, everything in heaven and on earth, in him.

Have you noticed how sometimes you have a story in the back of your mind which keeps peeping out even when you're talking about something else?

Imagine you've come back from work and the train has been late again. You stood for half an hour on the station platform getting cold and cross. Then when it arrived it was so full of people you had to stand, uncomfortably, all the way home.

But when you tell your family about the trip you find you're also telling them a larger story. Everybody knows that the trains aren't running properly because the present government has allowed them to get worse and worse so that they can have an excuse to introduce a new scheme of their own. But there's an election coming soon, and then you'll be able to vote out this government and put in another one that might at last get you a decent train service.

So as you talk about your anger over this evening's train ride, you are talking as well about your anger with the present government. And as you talk about how things could be better with the train you normally catch, you are talking as well about how good things are going to be with the new government. There is a larger framework, a larger story, within which your own smaller stories become more interesting and important.

Paul's great prayer at the opening of this letter is a celebration of the larger story within which every single Christian story – every story of individual conversion, faith, spiritual life, obedience and hope – is set. Only by understanding and celebrating the larger story can we hope to understand everything that's going on in our own smaller stories, and so observe God at work in and through our own lives.

The prayer itself falls into three sections, though each one is tied so closely to the others, and overlaid with so much praise and celebration, that sometimes it's difficult to see what's going on. Verses 4–6 are the first paragraph, following the introductory word of praise in verse 3. Verses 7–10 are the second, and verses 11–14 round the prayer off. Let's look at them in turn.

Verses 4–6 celebrate the fact that God's people in the Messiah are *chosen by grace*. This is, perhaps, the most mysterious thing of all. God, the creator, 'chose us in him', that is, in the king, 'before the world was made'; and he 'foreordained us for himself'.

Many people, including many devout Christians, have found this shocking, or even unbelievable. How can God choose some and not others? How can being a follower of Jesus Christ be a matter of God's prior decision, overriding any decision or freedom of our own?

Various answers can be given to this. We have to be careful here. Paul emphasizes throughout this paragraph that everything we have in Christ is a gift of God's grace; and in the next chapter he will declare that before this grace reached down to us we were 'dead', and needing to be 'made alive' (2.5). We couldn't lift a finger to help ourselves; the rescue we needed had to come from God's side. That's one of the things this opening section is celebrating.

The second thing, which is often missed in discussions of this point, is that our salvation in Christ is a vital stage, but only a stage, on the way to the much larger purpose of God. God's plan is for the whole cosmos, the entire universe; his choosing and calling of us, and his shaping and directing of us in the Messiah, are somehow connected with that larger intention.

This alerts us to the other hidden story which Paul is telling all through this great prayer. It is the story of the Exodus from Egypt. God chose Abraham, Isaac and Jacob to be the bearers of his promised salvation for the world – the rescue of the whole cosmos, humankind especially, from the sin and death that had come about through human rebellion. When Paul says that God chose *us* 'in Christ' – the 'us' here being the whole company of Christians, Jews and Gentiles alike – he is saying that those who believe in Jesus are now part of the fulfilment of that ancient purpose.

But the story, of course, doesn't stop there. In verses 7–10 Paul tells the story of the cross of Jesus in such a way that we can hear, underneath it, the ancient Jewish story of Passover. Passover was the night when the angel of death came through the land of Egypt, and the blood of the lamb sprinkled on the doorposts rescued the Israelites from the judgment that would otherwise have fallen on them. The word often used for that moment was 'redemption' or 'deliverance': it was the time when God went to Egypt and 'bought' for himself the people that had been enslaved there. Now, again in fulfilment of the old story, the true 'redemption' has occurred. Forgiveness of sins is the real 'deliverance' from the real slavemaster. And it's been accomplished through the sacrificial blood of Jesus.

Telling the story like this – the story of Jesus the Messiah, and the meaning of his death, told in such a way as to bring out the fact that it's the fulfilment of the Exodus story – is a classic Jewish way of celebrating the goodness of God. Worship, for Christians, will almost always involve *telling the story* of what God has done in and through Jesus. From the beginning, such storytelling built on the stories of God's earlier actions on Israel's behalf. The prayer will now conclude by moving forwards from the Christian version of the Exodus to the Christian version of the promised land.

THE INHERITANCE AND THE SPIRIT
Ephesians 1.11–14

[11]In him we have received the inheritance! We were foreordained to this, according to the intention of the one who does all things in accordance with the counsel of his purpose. [12]This was so that we, we who first hoped in the king, might exist for the praise of his glory. [13]In him you too, who heard the word of truth, the gospel of your salvation, and believed it – in him you were marked out with the spirit of promise, the holy one. [14]The spirit is the guarantee of our inheritance, until the time when the people who are God's special possession are finally reclaimed and freed. This, too, is for the praise of his glory.

Not far from where I was born there is an ancient castle. It stands imposingly, high above the banks of a river, defying anyone to attack it. These days, the likely attacks come from bank managers and tax-collectors rather than marauding raiders; so the owners have taken steps to use it profitably. The castle has become a wonderful spot for tourists to visit – and for movies to be made. Many historical films have included it, at least in the background. Part of one of the famous Harry Potter films was shot there.

It is still, though, a family home. The same family – one of Britain's ancient noble lines – has lived there for many centuries. It has been handed on from father to son. Or, in some cases, from brother to brother. Not long ago, the Duke who lived there died quite suddenly, in early middle age, and had no son or daughter to inherit. In a flash, his brother found himself thrown into the spotlight. All unexpectedly, he had received an inheritance which changed his life for ever.

He and his wife rose to the occasion. If they were going to have an inheritance like that, it was worth doing something with it. They decided to make the castle gardens among the most spectacular in the country and worked hard to realize their plans.

These days, an inheritance is often simply money – or something that can quickly be turned into money. But very often in the ancient world, and particularly in the Jewish world, an 'inheritance' consisted, like the castle and its grounds, of land that was not to be got rid of.

The basic inheritance that God had promised to Abraham, Isaac and Jacob was the land of Canaan. All the time that the Israelites were enslaved in Egypt, this was the hope that kept them going: the hope that, whatever the turns and twists of the plot in the long-running story, God himself would eventually give them the 'inheritance': not a gift of cash, but the ideal land, the land flowing with milk and honey.

Part of the meaning of the Exodus, therefore, was that they were now free to set off and go to claim their inheritance. They wandered in the wilderness for 40 years, led this way and that by the pillar of cloud by day and fire by night. The presence of the Holy One in their midst was dangerous – you would be foolish to grumble or rebel, as some of them found to their cost – but it was the guarantee that they would get there in the end. And they did.

In Ephesians Paul tells this part of the story over again, as the conclusion of his long opening act of worship and praise. Only this time, of course, it's the new Exodus, the new inheritance, and the new wilderness wandering. As often in his writings, he sees the church in the present age as doing again what Israel did in the desert: coming out of the slavery of sin through God's great action in Jesus the Messiah, and on the way to the new promised land.

But what is this new promised land? What is the promised inheritance?

The standard Christian answer for many years and in many traditions has been: 'Heaven'. Heaven, it has been thought, is the place to which we are going. Great books like John Bunyan's *Pilgrim's Progress* have been written in which the happy ending, rather than an inheritance suddenly received from a relative, is the hero reaching the end of this worldly life and going off to share the life of heaven. But that isn't what Paul says, here or elsewhere.

The inheritance he has in mind, so it appears from this passage, and the whole of chapter 1, is the whole world, when it's been renewed by a fresh act of God's power and love. Paul has already said in verse 10 that God's plan in the Messiah is to sum up everything in heaven and earth. God, after all, is the creator; he has no interest in leaving earth to rot and making do for all eternity with only one half of the original creation. God intends to flood the whole cosmos, heaven and earth together, with his presence and grace, and when that happens the new world that results, in which Jesus himself will be the central figure, is to be the 'inheritance' for which Jesus' people are longing.

At the moment, therefore, the people who in this life have come to know and trust God in Jesus are to be the signs to the rest of the world that this glorious future is on the way. Equally, the sign that they themselves have received which guarantees them their future is the holy spirit. The spirit is to the Christian and the church what the cloud and fire were in the wilderness: the powerful, personal presence of the living God, holy and not to be taken lightly, leading and guiding the often muddled and rebellious people to their inheritance.

But the spirit is more than just a leader and guide. The spirit is actually part of the promised inheritance, because the spirit is God's own presence, which in the new world will be fully and personally with us for ever. (That's why, in some New Testament visions of the future, such as Revelation 21, heaven and earth are joined together, so that 'the dwelling of God is with humans'.)

The spirit marks us out, stamps us with God's official seal, as the people in the present who are guaranteed to inherit God's new world.

KNOWING THE POWER OF THE KING

Ephesians 1.16–19

[16]I never stop giving thanks for you as I remember you in my prayers. [17]I pray that the God of King Jesus our Lord, the father of glory, would give you, in your spirit, the gift of being wise, of seeing things people can't normally see, because you are coming to know him [18]and to have the eyes of your inmost self opened to God's light. Then you will know exactly what the hope is that goes with God's call; you will know the wealth of the glory of his inheritance in his holy people; [19]and you will know the outstanding greatness of his power towards us who are loyal to him in faith, according to the working of his strength and power.

'So how strong is it?'

My friend was showing me his new telescope. It was set up in an upstairs room, looking out towards sea.

'Well, take a look.'

I had been scanning the horizon with my own small binoculars. There were a couple of ships going by. A few small fishing boats closer in. Nothing much else. I put my eye to his telescope and couldn't believe what I saw.

The two ships I had seen – suddenly they were so close that I could see their names on the side, and people walking to and fro on the deck. But that was only the beginning. Out beyond them, where my binoculars had registered nothing at all, were several other ships: large and small, military and commercial, including a cruise liner. The telescope seemed to have the uncanny power of making things appear out of nowhere.

Power is one of the great themes of Ephesians. Perhaps this is because Ephesus itself, and the surrounding area, was seen as a place of power. Certainly in social and civic terms the city was powerful, and was set to become more so. It was a major centre of imperial influence in Paul's day. The Roman emperors were keen to establish and maintain places where their rule could be celebrated and enhanced.

But it was also a centre of religious power. All sorts of cults and beliefs flourished, and frequently they focused on power: the power of what we might call magic, power to make things happen in the world, to influence people and events, to gain wealth or health or influence for yourself and to bring about the downfall of your enemies. Their world, in other words, was dominated by the 'principalities and powers', the various levels of rulers and authorities from local magistrates up to internationally recognized gods and goddesses, and all stages in between.

For Paul, the greatest display of power the world had ever seen took place when God raised Jesus from the dead (1.20). Nobody had ever been raised bodily from the dead, before or since. (If anybody today imagines that when the early Christians said Jesus had been raised from the dead, they meant that he had simply been exalted to heaven, they should think again. That wouldn't have been an extraordinary display of power, but rather the normal expectation of many, both Jews and non-Jews.) This power of the creator God at once sets itself apart from, and establishes itself as superior to, all the 'powers' that people might ever come across. The risen Jesus, in fact, is now enthroned, on the basis of this power of God, over the whole cosmos. And at the centre of Paul's prayer for the church in the area, which he now reports, is his longing that they will come to realize that this same power, the power seen at Easter and now vested in Jesus, is available to them for their daily use.

Far too many Christians today, and, one suspects, in Paul's day, are quite unaware that this power is there and is available. They are like I was with my friend: until I looked through his powerful telescope I simply didn't know what was out there. If someone says, 'Well, I don't seem to have much power as a

Christian,' or, 'I can't see the power of Jesus doing very much in the world,' that simply shows that they need this prayer of Paul. Paul doesn't imagine that all Christians will automatically be able to recognize the power of God. It will take, as he says in verse 17, a fresh gift of wisdom, of coming to see things people don't normally see. And this in turn will come about through knowing Jesus and having what Paul calls 'the eyes of your inmost self' opened to God's light.

God has already begun to work in them powerfully, as their loyal faith and love indicates (verse 15). So Paul can pray with confidence that God will now add this increase in wisdom and knowledge, especially in showing them two things: the inheritance, in all its glory, and the power of God which will bring it about in its proper time.

That power, the power which raised Jesus and which will transform the whole world and flood it with his glory, is in fact already available for us (verse 19). This doesn't mean we can become conjurors, performing spectacular tricks to impress people. Many of the things which God's power achieves in us, such as putting secret sins to death and becoming people of prayer, remain hidden from the world and even, sometimes, from other Christians.

GOD'S LOVE, GOD'S POWER – IN US
Ephesians 3.14–21

[14]Because of this, I am kneeling down before the father, [15]the one who gives the name of 'family' to every family that there is, in heaven and on earth. [16]My prayer is this: that he will lay out all the riches of his glory to give you strength and power, through his spirit, in your inner being; [17]that the king may make his home in your hearts, through faith; that love may be your root, your firm foundation; [18]and that you may be strong enough (with all God's holy ones) to grasp the breadth and length and height and depth, [19]and to know the king's love – though

actually it's so deep that nobody can really know it! So may God fill you with all his fullness.

[20]So: to the one who is capable of doing far, far more than we can ask or imagine, granted his power which is working in us – [21]to him be glory, in the church, and in King Jesus, to all generations, and to the ages of ages! Amen!

Love and power, power and love: these are the themes of perhaps two-thirds of the novels, plays and poems ever written. The love of power has laid waste continents and empires. The power of love has driven weak people to do powerful things – and, not infrequently, powerful people to do foolish things. These are the forces which shape our lives, our homes, our countries, our politics, our world. And these are the themes that run through the great prayer that Paul prays for the young Christians to whom he is writing.

One of the great Christian leaders of the late twentieth century, Archbishop Desmond Tutu of Cape Town, used to spend several hours in prayer very early in the morning. Nor was prayer then forgotten for the rest of the day. A friend of mine who travelled around with him described how, wherever they went, whatever new thing they were doing, Desmond would pause and pray.

The Western church has perhaps allowed itself to be lulled into thinking that prayer and action are at opposite ends of the scale of Christian activity. On the contrary. Those who want their actions to be effective for God's kingdom – as Desmond Tutu's undoubtedly were – should redouble their time and effort in prayer. Prayer brings together love and power: the relation of love that grows up between God and the person who prays, and the flowing of power from God to, and especially *through*, that person.

That is what Paul's prayer here is all about. Essentially, it is a prayer that the young Christians may discover the heart of what it means to be a Christian. It means knowing God as the all-loving, all-powerful father; it means putting down roots into that love – or, changing the picture, having that love as the rock-solid foundation for every aspect of one's life. It means having that love turn into a well-directed and effective energy in one's personal life. And it means the deep and powerful knowing and loving into which the Christian is invited to enter; or – to put the same thing another way – the knowing and loving which should enter into the Christian. Paul, quite clearly, knows all this in his own experience. He longs that those who have come to put their faith in Jesus should know it too.

At the heart of all this is a phrase which has become popular in the language of Christian experience: 'that the king may make his home in your hearts, through faith'. People talk easily, perhaps too easily, about 'inviting Jesus into your heart', or 'having Jesus in your heart'. The danger here is that it's easy for people, particularly when they are soaked in the culture of Western-style individualism, to imagine that being a Christian consists simply in being able to feel, or believe, that Jesus has somehow taken up residence within. In fact, Paul speaks far more often of Christians being 'in Christ' than of Christ being 'in Christians'. It's important to see our individual experience within the larger picture of our membership in God's family in the Messiah.

But of course, when that's been made clear, then it is also important that the living Lord, the king, should make his home within each Christian. That is what strengthens and renews us in our inner being (verse 16). That, as verse 17 implies, is what enables us to put down roots into God's love and to be built up as a secure, unmoveable house. That, as Paul says in the climax of the prayer in verses 18 and 19, will expand our mental and spiritual vision of the whole range of divine truth. Everything that might be offered in the fancy religions of Paul's day and ours (just this morning I came across a book offering new, secret knowledge which could apparently revolutionize my life, but which of course by-passed Jesus), all the ups and downs and to-ing and fro-ing, the breadth and length and depth and height, of knowledge whether human or divine – all is ours in the king and in his love. By having him in us, we are filled with all the fullness of God.

Once all this is in place, the results should start to emerge. Verses 20 and 21 are often used as a benediction in church services, and it's easy to see why. As we draw to the end of a time of prayer, the overarching aim should be to give God the glory. But if it's the true God we've been worshipping, we should be filled with a sense of new possibilities: of new tasks and new energy to accomplish them.

THANKS, JOY AND OVERFLOWING LOVE

Philippians 1.1–11

[1] From Paul and Timothy, slaves of King Jesus, to all God's holy ones in King Jesus who are in Philippi, together with the overseers and ministers: [2] grace to you and peace, from God our father and King Jesus the Lord.

[3] I thank my God every time I think of you! [4] I always pray with joy, whenever I pray for you all, [5] because of your partnership in the gospel from the first day until now. [6] Of this I'm convinced: the one who began a good work in you will thoroughly complete it by the day of King Jesus.

[7] It's right for me to think this way about all of you. You have me in your hearts, here in prison as I am, working to defend and bolster up the gospel. You are my partners in grace, all of you! [8] Yes: God can bear witness how much I'm longing for all of you with the deep love of King Jesus.

[9] And this is what I'm praying: that your love may overflow still more and more, in knowledge and in all astute wisdom. [10] Then you will be able to tell the difference between good and evil, and be sincere and faultless on the day of the Messiah, [11] filled to overflowing with the fruit of right living, fruit that comes through King Jesus to God's glory and praise.

Philippi, in northern Greece, was the first place in Europe that heard the news that there was a new king, namely the crucified and risen Jesus of Nazareth. You can read the story of Paul's first visit there in Acts 16. Paul's letter to the Philippians makes it clear that as he looked at all the churches he had founded, the people of Philippi were the ones who gave him most joy. To be sure, he loved them all; but this letter breathes a confident trust and enjoyment which we don't always find elsewhere. Now, in prison – almost certainly in Ephesus, since he speaks of coming to see them again (1.26), and in his other imprisonments he had no intention of returning to Greece – the Philippian church have sent him a gift of money. One of the reasons he's writing is to say a heartfelt 'Thank you'.

When people were put in prison in Paul's world, they were not normally given food by their captors; they had to rely on friends helping them. Since Paul probably couldn't carry on his tent-making business in prison, he was completely dependent on support like this. The fact that people from a different country would raise money, and send one of their number on the dangerous journey to carry it to an imprisoned friend, speaks volumes for the esteem and love in which they held him. People sometimes speak today as though Paul was an awkward, difficult, unpopular sort of person, but folk like that don't normally find this kind of support reaching them unbidden from friends far away.

This gives Paul added confidence when he prays for them, as he does constantly. He knows that when the gospel message of King Jesus does its life-changing work in people's hearts this isn't just a flash-in-the-pan 'religious experience' that might then fade away with the passing of time. If there is genuine faith in the risen Jesus, genuine loyalty to him as king, this can only be because the living God has worked, through the gospel, within people's hearts; and what God begins, he always finishes. This, of course, doesn't mean there aren't problems along the way; several of Paul's other letters, particularly 1 Corinthians, grapple with these. But Paul remains confident in the grace of God. Having begun the round-the-world journey of the work of salvation, God is going to complete it.

In this confidence, Paul prays for them; as so often, the opening of the letter looks ahead to what will come later by means of telling the recipients the content of his prayer for them. It has three elements.

First (verse 9), he prays that their love will overflow in knowledge and wisdom. This is not, perhaps, how we often think of love. We think of it as having to do with emotion and affection, not with knowledge and wisdom. For Paul they are all bound up together: what we call the 'heart' and what we call the 'head' were not separated, as we have sometimes allowed them to be. If Christian love is to be the genuine article – true love for God, true love for one another – it is bound to work its way out in a knowledge and wisdom which is more than mere book-learning. This kind of knowledge is a deep insight into the way God's world truly is, a knowledge open to everyone who is prepared to give themselves wholeheartedly in love to God through King Jesus.

Second (verse 10), he prays that this wise love will result in moral discernment. They lived, as we do, in a world where several moral issues were blurred and distorted, and it was often hard to see what was the right thing to do. Paul longs to see them grow in telling the difference between good and evil when so often they appear, at first glance, as shades of grey. That way, he says, they will approach the coming Day of the Lord, the king's great day, with confidence, because God will be transforming their whole lives into a holiness that goes beyond even the ritual purity demanded of priests in the Temple (the words he uses for 'sincere' and 'faultless' seem to carry that implication). This letter has quite a lot to say about the coming Day; and the main thing to say is that Christians can look forward to it with confidence and joy.

Finally (verse 11), he prays that they may be filled to overflowing with the fruit of right living. The word for 'right living' is another of Paul's big words. It's often translated 'righteousness', though that's not always a helpful word. It sometimes means God's own faithfulness, and sometimes the status of 'membership in

God's family', with all the privileges such as forgiveness of sins, which is God's gift to those who believe the gospel. Here it emphasizes more the behaviour which results from both God's faithfulness and the status of being forgiven family members. The important thing throughout is that at every stage of the process – when people first hear the gospel, when they believe it, when they begin to live by it, and when they make progress in faith and love – nothing is done to the glory of the people concerned, as though they were able arrogantly to advance their own cause. Everything is done, as he insists here, 'through King Jesus' and 'to the glory and praise of God'.

As usual, Paul's prayer for the church is a prayer that every church leader might wish to use for the people in their care. It's also a prayer that every Christian might use for himself or herself. And remember, as you use it: the reason you're praying it at all is that God has begun his good work in you all. And what God begins, he completes.

WISDOM AND GRATITUDE
Colossians 1.9–14

[9]For this reason, from the day we heard it, we haven't stopped praying for you. We're asking God to fill you with the knowledge of what he wants for you in all wisdom and spiritual understanding. [10]This will mean that you'll be able to conduct yourselves in a manner worthy of the Lord, and so give him real delight, as you bear fruit in every good work and grow up in the knowledge of God. [11]I pray that you'll be given all possible strength, according to the power of his glory, so that you'll have complete patience and become truly steadfast and joyful.

[12]And I pray that you will learn to give thanks to the father, who has made you fit to share the inheritance of God's holy ones in the light. [13]He has delivered us from the power of darkness, and transferred us into the kingdom of his beloved son. [14]He is the one in whom we have redemption, the forgiveness of sins.

We watched, holding our breath, as the mother duck left the pond at the head of her brood.

There were seven ducklings in all: four black ones and three yellow ones. They were lively and squeaky, scuttling to and fro. For days they had swum about with their mother in the little pond. Now it was time for her to take them to the nearby lake.

This meant danger. To get there they had to cross a main road and make their way through a park where dogs, cats, larger birds and several other predators would be watching. Fortunately, in this city at least, local residents are prepared for this moment and make sure that traffic comes to a stop to let the little procession pass through. They reached their destination safely. But we were left marvelling at the mother's apparent calm confidence as she led her little family through potential hazards and on to the larger world where she would then bring them up to maturity.

Paul, in prison in Ephesus, must often have felt like a mother duck. Here was he in a little church, just starting up, full of energy and enthusiasm but hardly yet aware of the great dangers and problems that were to be faced. He can't even be with them in person to guide them and teach them. The mother duck has to rely on instinct – her own, and that of her recently born babies – to see them through. But ordinary human instinct alone won't get the young church through to maturity. Human instincts are important, but they remain earthbound. When people become Christians, God implants into them a new sense of his presence and love, his guiding and strengthening. This sense needs nurturing and developing. New Christians need to understand what's happening to them, and how they must co-operate with the divine life that's gently begun to work in them.

Paul, in prison, can help this process in two ways: by writing, as he is doing, but supremely by prayer. He may not be with the Colossians in person. But the God who is with them is also with him, and in the mystery (and hard work) of prayer he can help their progress towards Christian maturity. That is what he's been doing; so, it appears later, has Epaphras (4.12–13). And in this paragraph he tells them what they have been praying for as they think of Colossae. Whether you're a new Christian yourself, needing to grow in the faith, or a Christian leader, wanting to nurture those in your care, Paul's prayer for the new church in Colossae provides a wonderful pattern.

The foundation of what he prays for is that the new Christian instinct may become firmly implanted in them. Just as the mother duck wants her brood to be able to work out for themselves how to feed, to avoid danger, and to live wisely in a threatening environment, so Paul longs to see young Christians coming to know for themselves what God's will is (verse 9). They need 'wisdom and spiritual understanding'; not just book-learning (though some of that may help) or human traditions (though they are often useful, too), but a deep inner sense of who they now are, of the newly created human life which they have received from God, and of what will nurture it or harm it. Christian teachers can talk till they're blue in the face, but unless their hearers have this inner sense of wisdom and understanding, this awareness of the true God loving them and shaping their lives in a new way, it won't produce genuine disciples.

With that in place, however, Paul's prayer passes to two other things: behaviour and bearing fruit (verse 10). The new instinct implanted in the Christian will lead him or her to a new lifestyle, which delights God not least because it reflects at last his glorious intention for his human creatures.

There are two lies which the world often tells about God's intention for human behaviour. First, people say that God doesn't want us to have a good time; second, they say that even if we try to live as he wants all we'll ever get is a grudging approval. People often imagine that God is eager to spot the slightest wrongdoing and tell us off for it. This verse shows how wrong both of these are. God's intention is for human life to flourish and bear fruit: what Paul said in verse 6 about the gospel, God's powerful word, he now says again about the people themselves in whose hearts and lives that word is doing its work. And when this happens God is personally delighted. Paul often declares that genuine Christian living gives God pleasure. It is we, with our little faith, who have imagined him to be grumpy and hard to please.

But if this is to happen, the new life that's been implanted in Christians has to show itself in the form of energy, power and strength to live in the new way. That, too, is promised, and that too is what Paul is praying for. God's power has already delivered us from the kingdom of darkness and transferred us into the kingdom of his son, Jesus. That same power is now available to continue the work of bringing our lives into conformity with the new world which opens up before us.

When Paul speaks of God rescuing people from one kingdom and giving them another one, and of 'redemption' and 'forgiveness' as the central themes of that rescue operation, he has the Exodus from Egypt in mind. What God has done in Jesus, and is now doing for them, is the new Exodus, the great moment of setting the slaves free. To become a Christian is to leave the 'Egypt' of sin and to travel gratefully towards the promised inheritance.

Why 'gratefully'? Because the climax of Paul's prayer is that the young Christians will learn the art of thanksgiving. He will, in fact, mention this over and over again; it's a central theme of the whole letter. What Paul most wants to see growing in the church, as a sign of healthy Christian life on the way to maturity, is gratitude to God for the extraordinary things he's done in Jesus, and the remarkable things he is continuing to do in the world and in their lives.

Spontaneous gratitude of this kind is a sign that they are coming to know and love the true God, as opposed to some imaginary one. Gods that people invent can't compare with the true one when it comes to overflowing generosity. Paul would say to us, as he said to the young Christians in Colossae, that a life lived in the presence of this God will be a life full of thanksgiving. Or have we forgotten who our God really is?

WORDS OF BLESSING

1 Thessalonians 3.11–13

[11]Now may God himself, our father, and our Lord Jesus, steer us on our way to you. [12]And may the Lord make your love for one another, and for everybody, abound and overflow, just as ours does for you. [13]That way, your hearts will be strengthened and kept blameless in holiness before God our father when our Lord Jesus is present again with all his holy ones. Amen.

When children begin to learn a musical instrument, or to sing, the teacher often plays alongside them. The children hear the music from the teacher mixed in with the sounds they are making, and this encourages them to work together, to copy the teacher and make the same noises. It will take time, of course; and often the noise of youthful music-making is some way from being pleasant to listen to on its own, or even with a teacher. But as children grow in confidence, they move step by step towards the day when they can play without the teacher there, and may even in due course become teachers themselves.

So it is with prayer. By ourselves we have an instinct to pray, just as many people have an instinct for making music. But if this is left untaught and unguided, it will often produce the equivalent, in prayer, of the adult whose music-making consists of picking out a few tunes on a piano with one finger, or of singing only the easiest of tunes. Better than nothing, of course; but how much better to be able to make the music you are really capable of! And how much better, in learning to pray, to grow beyond a few short childish sentences, or the emergency prayers that we find ourselves praying when we are in trouble, and to become real grown-up praying people, able in due course to help others too.

So what can we learn from this short but deep prayer of Paul's?

First, we learn that prayer is grounded in the life and work of God himself – the God we come to know, through Jesus, as father. Twice in this short prayer Paul draws together God the father and Jesus the Lord, and there are signs throughout his writing that this was one of his regular ways of thinking about and addressing God and Jesus together. This isn't simply a matter of getting the labels right for the God we are talking to. Prayer that is grounded in the character of God, as revealed in Jesus, is prayer that is learning to depend on the goodness, the generosity, the sovereign love, of this God as they are unveiled in Jesus' saving death and triumphant resurrection. Prayer, at its very heart, is an exploration into the heart and character of God himself, not so much for the sake of enjoying being there (though that will come, too) but for the sake of bringing before this God the church and the world that need his healing love.

Prayer that acknowledges this God, this Lord, is prayer that will grow in confidence. If God is truly God, and if Jesus is truly the Lord of the world, we don't pray like people who are hoping that this God, this Lord, may somehow be able to pull off a clever move despite the power of other gods and lords. We pray with confidence to the one who is supreme over all, and who can do far more than all we can ask or think (Ephesians 3.20).

Prayer of this sort is also prayer with a future reference. It knows that this God intends one day to bring heaven and earth together in a new way, with the personal presence of Jesus as the central feature of this new world. Jesus will come again, 'and all his holy ones with him'; this is a quotation from one of the great Old Testament statements of hope (Zechariah 14.5), which Paul takes as referring to the final appearing of Jesus and all those who belong to him. The Lord's Prayer, too, has a strong future dimension: when we pray for daily bread, for forgiveness, and for deliverance from evil, we do so having already prayed for God's kingdom to come. Thus Paul's prayer for his own plans to visit northern Greece again, for the church to become a place where love is so plentiful that it seems to be overflowing from every corner, and for the Christians to be established with blameless and holy hearts – these are not simply miscellaneous requests. They focus on things that will make full sense at the great coming day of the presence of God and of Jesus.

Focused on God; looking eagerly towards God's future; and praying, in effect, for the work of God's spirit in the present. Some have wondered where the spirit is when Paul mentions God and Jesus so closely and frequently together. The proper answer is that the spirit is the one who is inspiring the prayer itself in Paul and his friends, and who is the hidden agency at work in the church to produce the results God and his people long to see. It is the spirit who enables Christians to love one another, and those outside the church, with a love whose supply never dries up no matter what demands are made on it. It is the spirit who settles the hearts of God's people to strive after holiness, to live without blame before God, and to become established and strengthened in that way of life. It is the spirit who is at work in the present to prepare all God's people to be what he wants them to be when he appears again.

What will happen if we make Paul's prayer a pattern for our own? Can we listen for the tunes he's playing, and begin to play them alongside him?

6

OTHER EARLY CHRISTIAN PRAYERS

MARY'S SONG OF PRAISE
Luke 1.39–55

[39]Mary got up then and there, and went in excitement to the hill country of Judaea. [40]She went into Zechariah's house, and greeted Elisabeth. [41]When Elisabeth heard Mary's greeting, the baby gave a leap in her womb. Elisabeth was filled with the holy spirit, [42]and shouted at the top of her voice: 'Of all women, you're the blessed one! And the fruit of your womb – he's blessed, too! [43]Why should this happen to me, that the mother of my Lord should come to me? [44]Look – when the sound of your greeting came to my ears, the child in my womb gave a great leap for joy! [45]A blessing on you, for believing that what the Lord said to you would come true!'

[46]Mary said,

'My heart declares that the Lord is great,
[47]my spirit exults in my saviour, my God.
[48]He saw his servant-girl in her humility;
from now, I'll be blessed by all peoples to come.
[49]The Powerful One, whose name is Holy,
has done great things for me, for me.
[50]His mercy extends from father to son,
from mother to daughter for those who fear him.
[51]Powerful things he has done with his arm:
he routed the arrogant through their own cunning.
[52]Down from their thrones he hurled the rulers,
up from the earth he raised the humble.
[53]The hungry he filled with the fat of the land,
but the rich he sent off with nothing to eat.
[54]He has rescued his servant, Israel his child,

because he remembered his mercy of old,
[55]just as he said to our long-ago ancestors –
Abraham and his descendants for ever.'

What would make you celebrate wildly, without inhibition?

Perhaps it would be the news that someone close to you who'd been very sick was getting better and would soon be home.

Perhaps it would be the news that your country had escaped from tyranny and oppression, and could look forward to a new time of freedom and prosperity.

Perhaps it would be seeing that the floods which had threatened your home were going down again.

Perhaps it would be the message that all your money worries, or business worries, had been sorted out and you could relax.

Perhaps it would be the telephone call to say that you had been appointed to the job you'd always longed for.

Whatever it might be, you'd do things you normally wouldn't.

You might dance round and round with a friend.

You might shout and throw your hat in the air (I once did that without thinking, before I stopped to reflect what a cliché it was).

You might telephone everybody you could think of and invite them to a party.

You might sing a song. You might even make one up as you went along – probably out of snatches of poems and songs you already knew, or perhaps by adding your own new words to a great old hymn.

And if you lived in any kind of culture where rhythm and beat mattered, it would be the sort of song you could clap your hands to, or stamp on the ground.

Now read Mary's song like that. (It's often called *Magnificat*, because that is its first word in Latin.) It's one of the most famous songs in Christianity. It's been whispered in monasteries, chanted in cathedrals, recited in small remote churches by evening candlelight, and set to music with trumpets and kettledrums by Johann Sebastian Bach.

It's the gospel before the gospel, a fierce bright shout of triumph thirty weeks before Bethlehem, thirty years before Calvary and Easter. It goes with a swing and a clap and a stamp. It's all about God, and it's all about revolution. And it's all because of Jesus – Jesus who's only just been conceived, not yet born, but who has made Elisabeth's baby leap for joy in her womb and has made Mary giddy with excitement and hope and triumph. In many cultures today, it's the women who really know how to celebrate, to sing and dance, with their bodies and voices saying things far deeper than words. That's how Mary's song comes across here.

Yes, Mary will have to learn many other things as well. A sword will pierce her soul, she is told when Jesus is a baby. She will lose him for three days when he's twelve. She will think he's gone mad when he's thirty. She will despair completely for a further three days in Jerusalem, as the God she now wildly celebrates seems to have deceived her (that, too, is part of the same Jewish tradition she draws on in this song). All of us who sing her song should remember these things too. But the moment of triumph will return with Easter and Pentecost, and this time it won't be taken away.

Why did Mary launch into a song like this? What has the news of her son got to do with God's strong power overthrowing the power structures of the world, demolishing the mighty and exalting the humble?

Mary and Elisabeth shared a dream. It was the ancient dream of Israel: the dream that one day all that the prophets had said would come true. One day Israel's God would do what he had said to Israel's earliest ancestors: all nations would be blessed through Abraham's family. But for that to happen, the powers that kept the world in slavery had to be toppled. Nobody would normally thank God for blessing if they were poor, hungry, enslaved and miserable. God would have to win a victory over the bullies, the power-brokers, the forces of evil which people like Mary and Elisabeth knew all too well, living as they did in the dark days of Herod the Great, whose casual brutality was backed up with the threat of Rome. Mary and Elisabeth, like so many Jews of their time, searched the scriptures, soaked themselves in the psalms and prophetic writings which spoke of mercy, hope, fulfilment, reversal, revolution, victory over evil, and of God coming to the rescue at last.

All of that is poured into this song, like a rich, foaming drink that comes bubbling over the edge of the jug and spills out all round. Almost every word is a biblical quotation such as Mary would have known from childhood. Much of it echoes the song of Hannah in 1 Samuel 2, the song which celebrated the birth of Samuel and all that God was going to do through him. Now these two mothers-to-be celebrate together what God is going to do through their sons, John and Jesus.

This is all part of Luke's scene-setting for what will follow, as the two boys grow up and really do become the agents of God's long-promised revolution, the victory over the powers of evil. Much of Mary's song is echoed by her son's preaching, as he warns the rich not to trust in their wealth, and promises God's kingdom to the poor.

Underneath it all is a celebration of God. God has taken the initiative – God the Lord, the saviour, the Powerful One, the Holy One, the Merciful One, the Faithful One. God is the ultimate reason to celebrate.

LOOK UPON THEIR THREATS

Acts 4.23–31

²³When they had been released, they went back to their own people, and told them everything that the chief priests and the elders had said. ²⁴When they heard it, they all together lifted up their voices to God.

'Sovereign Master,' they said, 'you made heaven and earth, and the sea, and everything in them. ²⁵And you said through the holy spirit, by the mouth of our ancestor David, your servant,

'Why did the nations fly into a rage,
and why did the peoples think empty thoughts?
²⁶The kings of the earth arose
and the rulers gathered themselves together
against the Lord and against his anointed Messiah.

²⁷'It's true: Herod and Pontius Pilate, together with the nations and the peoples of Israel, gathered themselves together in this very city against your holy child Jesus, the one you anointed, ²⁸to do whatever your hand and your plan had foreordained to take place. ²⁹So now, Master, look on their threats; and grant that we, your servants, may speak your word with all boldness, ³⁰while you stretch out your hand for healing, so that signs and wonders may come about through the name of your holy child Jesus.'

³¹When they had prayed, the place where they were gathered was shaken. They were all filled with the holy spirit, and they boldly spoke the word of God.

In the early summer of 1989, I went to Jerusalem to teach, and to work on a couple of books, one of which was about Jesus himself. One day, sitting in my borrowed room at St George's Cathedral, I was struggling with a few pages I was trying to write, concerning the battles Jesus had over his exorcisms – the battles, that is, both with the demons themselves and with the people who were accusing him of being, himself, in league with the devil. I was conscious, as I was struggling with this material, that it was not only difficult to say what had to be said historically, but that it was difficult to get it straight theologically, and that in attempting both tasks I was myself straying into a field of forces which I would have preferred to avoid.

Suddenly, just as I had got down onto the computer a few paragraphs in which I had at last said what I wanted to say, there was a loud bang. All the electric systems in the building went dead. A workman downstairs, trying to fix something else, had put a nail straight through a main cable. He was lucky to be alive. And I had lost my morning's work.

It was such a shock, after my hours of silent struggle with the text, the history and the meanings, that I almost burst into tears. I went next door, sat down at the piano, and played for a few minutes to calm myself down and clear my head. Then I came back into my room and knelt down at the prayer desk. For some reason (perhaps I had heard them in the cathedral earlier that day, or that week) the words of Acts 4.29 came straight into my head.

'Now, Lord,' I prayed, 'look upon their threats; and grant to your servant to speak your word with all boldness, while you stretch out your hand to heal, and signs and wonders are performed in the name of your holy child Jesus.' I went back to the desk and reconstructed the morning's work.

I have prayed that prayer many times, not usually in such dramatic circumstances, but often with a sense that today, just as much as in the apostles' time, there is a battle going on. Sometimes it is with actual, official authorities, as in Acts 4. Sometimes it is with the spirit of the age, with the implied mood of an organization, a family or a club, where certain things are done and said and certain other things are emphatically 'not done' or 'not said' – including, it may be, a definite statement of Christian truth, which bursts upon a room in such circumstances like someone saying a rude word. Sometimes the battle is internal, where things I badly want to do, say or think conflict with what the text really is saying, and I have to recognize my own bias, repent and allow the text to reform my outlook and behaviour. Whatever, the battle is real. I do not say it is always necessarily with actual dark powers, though I would never rule that out. I just know that when you come to speak or write about Jesus, about his cross, about his resurrection, about the new life which can break chains and set people free, there seem to be powers around the place which do their best to oppose what you are doing.

In this passage we see just how important the Psalms were for the early church as it faced opposition from the authorities. We find the apostles at prayer, returning to their friends after a trip to the Temple which, against expectations, had gone on from one afternoon to the next morning. The Psalm they focus on is Psalm 2: a spectacular poem, full of meaning relevant for exactly this situation.

Psalm 2 begins by questioning, before God, why the nations are in such an uproar, and the rulers scheming and plotting. This question stands within a long Jewish tradition in which God places his chosen people amidst the warring and violent nations of the earth, as a sign of his coming kingdom, the sovereign rule by which he will eventually bring peace and justice to the world. And on this occasion the means by which God will do this is through his anointed King, the one who will be hailed as 'son of God'. To this 'son of God', declares the Psalm, God will give not just the promised land as his inheritance, but all the nations of the world. The promises to Abraham have been extended, rather as in Psalm 72 or Psalm 89, and now they embrace the whole world.

So when the apostles quote Psalm 2 in their confident, exhilarated prayer in verses 25 and 26 they are not just finding a vague proof-text to help them anchor a general sense that all the world is against them. They are calling up a very specific text which speaks graphically and powerfully of the Messiah as the son of God, destined to rule the whole world. Woven deep into the heart of early Christian belief was exactly this note, as we find in a passage in Paul. In Romans 1.3–5, where he may be drawing on an early Christian confession of faith, he declares that in the resurrection God demonstrated that Jesus really was his son, the Messiah from the seed of David, and that this Jesus was therefore the Lord of the whole world, claiming allegiance from all people.

Praying like this is confident praying, not because people necessarily feel more devout than at other times, but because they are rooting themselves firmly in the ancient tradition of scripture. They start their prayer by invoking God as the creator of heaven, earth, the sea and everything else – the God, in other words, of the Old Testament, the God who can be appealed to for all that takes place within his domains. Then follows the quote from the Psalm. Then the present situation is placed firmly on the map of the scriptural story which has already been celebrated. As a result, the prayer can acknowledge the strong theological point that even the apparently disastrous things that took place as Jesus went to the cross were not outside God's will (verse 28). The wickedness of rulers is held in check by, and contained within, the overall purpose of God, who makes even human wrath turn to his praise.

With the ground thus prepared, the main triple thrust of the prayer is quite straightforward. Not 'Lord, please cause them to die horribly' or 'Please stop them being so unpleasant.' Not 'Lord, let this persecution stop,' or even 'Please convert the authorities, so that your work can go forward.' Rather, quite simply, 'Now, Lord, look on their threats; let us go on speaking boldly; and will you please continue to work powerfully.' The opposition are there, and God knows about them. We are here, and we need to be faithful, to continue to speak of Jesus boldly and confidently. And here is the power of God, which is not in our possession but which, because of Jesus, will continue to be at work to set up signposts pointing people to the new thing which is happening through him.

The church needs to learn, in every generation, what it means to pray with confidence like this. We do not go looking for persecution. But when it comes, in whatever form, it certainly concentrates the mind, sends us back to the scriptures, and casts us on God's mercy and power. The church needs, again and again, that sense of God's powerful presence, shaking us up, blowing away the cobwebs, filling us with the spirit, and giving us that same boldness.

THE GOD OF PEACE

Hebrews 13.20–21

[20]May the God of peace, who led up from the dead our Lord Jesus, the great shepherd of the sheep, through the blood of the

> eternal covenant, [21]make you complete in every good work so
> that you may do his will. May he perform, in you, whatever will
> be pleasing in his sight, through Jesus the Messiah. Glory be to
> him for ever and ever, Amen!

This great blessing, the crowning glory of the final passage of the
letter to the Hebrews, is still used regularly in many churches,
especially in the Easter season. The writer has not, up to this
point, made much of the actual resurrection of Jesus, though
he has assumed it throughout. He has chosen to concentrate
more on his sacrificial death on the one hand, and his going on
our behalf into the heavenly sanctuary on the other. But both of
these only make the sense they do because Jesus was raised from
the dead, as the whole New Testament insists on page after page.
And here, in drawing together the lines of thought in the letter
as a whole, this finally becomes explicit.

God 'led up' Jesus, back from the world of the dead, demonstrating that he was indeed 'the great shepherd of the sheep'. His
blood, shed on the cross, has become the sacrificial blood which
inaugurates the new covenant, the ultimate bond between God
and his people, the agreement between them which brings in the
'age to come' for which Israel had longed. That's what 'eternal'
really means: not just 'going on for ever and ever' (which sometimes sounds a bit boring), but 'in relation to God's new age', in
which there will be new tasks, new possibilities, new creative
challenges.

Nor do we have to wait for 'life after death' for these to begin.
God desires to accomplish them, at least in a preliminary way,
through his people even in the present. That's why this blessing
goes on to pray that God will 'make you complete in every good
work so that you may do his will' (verse 21). When someone is
getting ready to do a great task, they are trained up and kitted
out for it, whether it's a lawyer getting ready to work in the
courtroom, a plumber needing all the tools of the trade or a
bishop getting ready to take on responsibility for part of God's

church. Hebrews is praying that, whatever task each Christian is called to undertake, God will equip him or her fully for it, not only outwardly but also inwardly, so that he or she will 'perform', or accomplish, whatever will be pleasing in his sight.

Here we are at the heart of the mystery of Christian living, Christian leadership and Christian work for the kingdom. It is quite clear from the whole letter that to engage in such work requires effort, determination and patience. The fact that God is at work within us, as individuals and as communities, doesn't take that away. But, as we prepare for the work, engage in it and thank God for it when it's done, we must never forget that it is, ultimately, something that he does, mysteriously, in and through us.

Like Jesus himself, we may have to undergo great struggles as we learn what this means in practice (5.7–9). Indeed, if it really is 'through Jesus' that God is at work in us, we should expect that this will be the case. All the more reason, then, from start to finish, to give him 'glory for ever and ever'. He is the one who pioneered the way, who makes it possible for us to enter even now into God's very presence, and who waits to welcome us to the city that is to come. He is also the one through whom, because of his death, resurrection and ascension, and because of the gift of his own spirit, we are enabled to do and to be what we are called to do and to be, and to face the consequences with joy.

All this and more is summed up in the closing greeting in verse 25: grace be with you.

TO THE ONE AND ONLY GOD

Judah 24–25

[24]Now to the one who is able to keep you standing upright, and to present you before his glory, undefiled and joyful – [25]to the one and only God, our saviour through Jesus the Messiah our Lord, be glory, majesty, power and authority before all the ages, and now, and to all the ages to come. Amen.

Judah's instincts as a writer grow straight out of his instincts as a Christian: that whatever joys and sorrows have come to pass, all must in the end be gathered up again in praise to the one true God. The form his concluding praise takes embodies in itself, in verse 24: the God who deserves all praise is 'the one who is able to keep you standing upright'.

Many translations put this more negatively, 'to keep you from falling'. That expresses truth as well, but the word Judah uses is a bit more positive: 'to keep you unstumbling'. The image is of someone walking along who might have tripped over, but has not done so in fact. That is what we should pray for, and that is what we should praise God for when it happens.

And the unstumbling walk is going towards a definite destination. The goal towards which we are moving is that moment when we shall be presented before God's glory, undefiled and joyful. The letter has had much to say about defilement, and the whole tone has been gloomy as a result. Looking into the murky pit of human wickedness is always like that. The alternative to the licentious and Jesus-denying teaching of the infiltrators isn't, though, a gloomy, kill-joy religion. The very opposite! It is about glory, about purity, about glad and thrilling celebration. This, after all, is what we were made for.

Judah then gathers the whole thing up in one of the all-time classic bursts of Christian praise, praise which wells up when the holy spirit has flooded the heart with the knowledge of God in Jesus and of the rescue which he has accomplished.

PRAISE TO THE CREATOR

Revelation 4.6b–11

[6b]In the middle of the throne, and all around the throne, were four living creatures, full of eyes in front and behind. [7]The first creature was like a lion, the second creature was like an ox, the third creature had a human face, and the fourth creature was

like a flying eagle. ⁸Each of the four creatures had six wings, and they were full of eyes all round and inside. Day and night they take no rest, as they say,

> Holy, holy, holy,
> Lord God Almighty,
> Who Was and Who Is and Who Is to Come.

⁹When the creatures give glory and honour and thanksgiving to the one who is sitting on the throne, the one who lives for ever and ever, ¹⁰the twenty-four elders fall down in front of the one who is sitting on the throne, and worship the one who lives for ever and ever. They throw down their crowns in front of the throne, saying, ¹¹'O Lord our God, you deserve to receive glory and honour and power, because you created all things; because of your will they existed and were created.'

Scientists and anthropologists have often asked themselves, 'What is it that humans can do that computers can't do?' Computers, after all, can play chess better than most of us. They can work out answers to all kinds of questions that would take us a lot longer. Some people have boldly declared that, though at the moment computers can't do quite everything that we can, they will one day overtake us.

The writer David Lodge wrote a powerful novel on this theme, entitled *Thinks . . .* The heroine eventually discovers the answer: humans can weep; and humans can forgive. Those are two very powerful and central human activities. They take place in a quite different dimension from anything a computer can do. But without them, we would be less than human.

A similar question is often posed: 'What can humans do that animals can't do?' Again, some scientists have tried to insist that we humans are simply 'naked apes', a more sophisticated version perhaps, but still within the same continuum. This is a trickier question than the one about computers, but to get straight to the point: in our present passage, the main difference is that humans can say the word 'because'. In particular, they can say it about God himself.

Consider the two songs of praise in this passage, the first in verse 8 and the second in verse 11. The first one is the song which the four living creatures sing round the clock, day and night. They praise God as the holy one; they praise him as the everlasting one. The four creatures deserve our attention for other reasons, too. They seem in some ways to resemble the seraphim who surround God in Isaiah's vision in the Temple (Isaiah chapter 6), and they are also quite like the four creatures of Ezekiel's vision (Ezekiel 1). They represent the animal creation, including humans but at this stage with the human-faced creature being simply one among the others, alongside the king of the wild beasts (the lion), the massive leader of tamed animals (the ox), and the undisputed king of the birds (the eagle). (In some early Christian traditions, these animals represent the four gospel writers, so that Matthew (the human face), Mark (the lion), Luke (the ox) and John (the eagle) are thought of as the living creatures who surround, and worship, the Jesus of whom they speak.) These remarkable creatures seem to be not merely surrounding God's throne but ready to do his bidding. Twice John tells us that they are 'full of eyes': unsleeping, keeping watch for God over his whole creation.

The song of these living creatures is simply an act of adoring praise. We are meant, reading this passage, to see with the Psalmist that all creation is dependent on God and worships him in its own way. That alone is worth pondering as a striking contrast to how most of us view the animal kingdom. But the contrast with the twenty-four elders is then made all the more striking. Creation as a whole simply worships God; the humans who represent God's people *understand why they do so*. 'You *deserve*,' they say, 'to receive glory and honour and power, *because* you created all things.' There it is: the 'because' that distinguishes humans from other animals, however noble those animals may be in their own way. Humans are given the capacity to reflect, to understand what's going on. And, in particular, to express that understanding in worship.

Worship, after all, is the most central human activity. Certainly it's the most central Christian activity. When I was a student, many of us busied ourselves with all kinds of Christian activities – teaching and learning, studying scripture, evangelism, prayer meetings and so on. We went to church quite a lot, but never (I think) reflected much on what we were doing there. There was, after all, a sermon to learn from, and the hymns were good teaching aids as well. It was a time of learning and fellowship. When a friend suggested at one point that worship was actually the centre of everything, the rest of us looked at him oddly. It seemed a bit of a cop-out.

Now, of course, I know he was right. Worship is what we were made for; worship with a *because* in it is what marks us out as genuine human beings.

Perhaps this is something on which we should reflect carefully. Do we, in our private prayers and worship, and in our public services and liturgies, give sufficient weight to praising God as the creator of all things? In particular, are we conscious of our vocation to worship with a 'because'? Do we (in other words) allow our thinking about God to inform our praise? Do we think through the fact that he *deserves* 'glory, honour and power' because of what he has done?

All this may seem rather obvious. But actually it's anything but. The world has been full of movements, systems, philosophies and religions that have ignored creation as shabby, or irrelevant to 'spiritual' life, or that have vilified it as a nasty, dark and dangerous place, full of evil and death. Equally, the world has been full of movements which, instead of worshipping the God who made the world, have worshipped the world itself, or forces within it (money, sex, war, power – the usual lot). Revelation sets out the delicate but decisive balance. All creation worships God; we humans are called to worship him with mind as well as heart, recognizing that he is worthy of all praise as the creator of all things.

WORTHY IS THE LAMB!

Revelation 5.8–14

[8]When he took the scroll, the four living creatures and the twenty-four elders fell down in front of the lamb. They each had a harp, and they each had golden bowls full of incense, which are the prayers of God's holy people. [9]They sing a new song, which goes like this:

> You are worthy to take the scroll;
> you are worthy to open its seals;
> for you were slaughtered and with your own blood
> you purchased a people for God,
> from every tribe and tongue,
> from every people and nation
> [10]and made them a kingdom and priests to our God
> and they will reign on the earth.

[11]As I watched, I heard the voice of many angels around the throne, the living creatures and the elders. Their number was ten thousand times ten thousand, thousands upon thousands, [12]and they were saying in full voice,

> The slaughtered lamb has now deserved
> to take the riches and the power,
> to take the wisdom, strength and honour,
> to take the glory, and the blessing.

[13]Then I heard every creature in heaven, on the earth, under the earth, and in the sea, and everything that is in them, saying,

> To the One on the throne and the lamb
> be blessing and honour and glory
> and power for ever and ever!

[14]'Amen!' cried the four living creatures. As for the elders, they fell down and worshipped.

Think of it as a visit to the theatre. You are sitting in the dark when the drum begins. A slow, steady rhythm. It's telling you something. It's going somewhere. It builds up, louder and louder. Then the voices join in. Wild, excited singing, rich and vivid. That too builds up, louder and louder. Then, as the stage lights come on, the musicians join in as well: the rich brass, the shimmering strings, the sharp, clear oboe and the flute fluttering like a bird to and fro over the top of it all. The music is designed to set the scene, to open the play, to make you realize that this is drama like you've never seen it before.

And the actors? Now for the shock. John, in describing this scene, has hinted that *we are the actors*. We are listening to the music so that we can now come on stage, ready or not, and play our part.

It's there in the opening of the music that he describes. When the elders fall down in front of the lamb, each of them was holding two things: a harp, and a golden bowl of incense. John tells us what the incense is: it's the prayers of God's people, that is, of you and me. The heavenly scene is umbilically related to the earthly. The ordinary, faithful, humble prayers of Christians here on earth appear in heaven as glorious, sweet-smelling incense. I suspect the same is true of the music, with the heavenly harps corresponding to the song, however feeble and out of tune, which we sing to God's praise here and now. Then, in the first of the three songs in this passage, we find that the lamb is being praised, not just for rescuing us but for turning us from hopeless rebels into useful servants, from sin-slaves into 'a kingdom and priests'. From rubbish into royalty. This is our play. The lamb has set us free to stop being spectators and to start being actors.

We hear this crescendo of songs, then, not merely with excitement and eager fascination but with a sense of vocation. First, the praise of the lamb for what he's done (verses 9 and 10): he is indeed worthy to take and open the scroll and its seals. He is worthy (that is) to be the agent to carry forward God's plan to destroy the destroyers, to thwart the forces of evil, to confront the seemingly all-powerful and to establish his new order instead. And the way the lamb has done this is through his own death, his own blood.

Any first-century Jew would know that this meant 'through his death seen as a sacrifice'. Similarly, they would know that a sacrifice through which God 'purchased a people ... to be a kingdom and priests' is the ultimate Passover sacrifice, the final fulfilment of what God had done close up in history when he set his people free from their slavery in Egypt, 'purchasing' them like slaves from a slave-market, in order to establish them as a 'royal priesthood', as the people through whom he would accomplish his worldwide purposes. That much is clear in the book of Exodus (19.4–6).

But John, as so often, isn't just evoking one biblical passage. This first song also echoes the great passage in Daniel 7 where, after the raging of the monsters and the vindication of 'one like a son of man', God establishes his rule over the whole earth in and through the 'people of the holy ones of the Most High' (7.22, 27). The rescue effected in Daniel is, as it were, the great new Exodus, with the monsters who have oppressed God's people taking the place of Pharaoh in Egypt. John is picking up the same storyline, only now putting together the slaughtered Passover lamb and the vindicated son of man. This breathtaking move is made possible, indeed obvious, by the rushing together of both vocations in Jesus himself.

The first song, then, praises the lamb for rescuing a people by his death so that they could then take forward God's royal and redemptive purposes ('kingdom and priests') for the wider world. The second song, in which thousands upon thousands of angels join, turns from what the lamb has *achieved* to what he has *deserved*, namely, all the honour and glory of which creation is capable. The wealth and strength of the nations belongs to him; everything that ennobles and enriches human life, everything that enables people to live wisely, to enjoy and celebrate the goodness of God's world – all this is to be laid at his feet.

Sadly, there are many Christians who think of Jesus purely in terms of their own comfort and hope ('he has rescued us; he is with us as a friend') and who fail completely to see the sheer scope of his majesty, the sweep of his glory. Many rest content to have Jesus around the place for particular 'spiritual' purposes, but continue to assign riches, power, glory and the rest to earthly forces and rulers. Perhaps one of the reasons why Revelation is marginalized in some churches is precisely because it so strongly challenges this attitude.

And so to the third song, in which every creature in every part of God's creation joins in, much as in Paul's vision in Philippians 2.9–11. This time the praise of the lamb has been joined together with the praise of God the creator, as in chapter 4. In thunderous worship the whole creation praises 'the One on the throne and the lamb'.

This is John's own way of glimpsing and communicating the mind-challenging but central truth at the heart of Christian faith: Jesus, the lion-lamb, Israel's Messiah, the true man – this Jesus shares the worship which belongs, and uniquely and only belongs, to the one creator God.

But notice what this means. The affirmation of the full, unequivocal divinity of the lion-lamb comes, and only comes, in the context of the victory of God, through the lion-lamb, over all the powers of evil. It isn't enough just to agree with the idea, in the abstract, that Jesus is, in some sense or other, God. (People often say to me, 'Is Jesus God?', as though we knew who 'God' was ahead of time, and could simply fit Jesus in to that picture.) God is the creator, who is intimately involved with his world, and worshipped by that world. God has plans and purposes to deliver his world from all that has spoiled it; in other words, to re-establish his sovereign rule, his 'kingdom', on earth as in heaven. It is at the heart of those plans, and only there, that we find the lion-lamb sharing the throne of the one God. The church has all too often split off a bare affirmation of Jesus' 'divinity' from an acceptance of God's kingdom-agenda. To do so is to miss the point, and to use a version of one part of the truth as a screen to stop oneself from having to face the full impact of the rest of the truth. We discover, and celebrate, the divinity of the lion-lamb Messiah only when we find ourselves caught up to share his work as the royal priesthood, summing up creation's praises before him but also bringing his rescuing rule to bear on the world.

THE SONG OF THE LAMB

Revelation 15.1–4

¹Then I saw another sign – a great, amazing sight in heaven: seven angels who were bringing the seven last plagues. With them God's anger is completed. ²And I saw what looked like a sea of glass, mixed with fire. There, by that glassy sea, stood the people who had won the victory over the monster and over its image, and over the number of its name. They were holding harps of God, ³and they were singing the song of Moses the servant of God, and the song of the lamb. This is how it went:

> Great and amazing are your works,
> O Lord God, the Almighty one.
> Just and true are your ways,
> O King of the nations.
> ⁴Who will not fear you, Lord,
> and glorify your name?
> For you alone are holy.
> For all nations shall come
> and worship before you,
> because your judgments have been revealed.

What is it that attracts people to the Christian message? What is it that draws them to worship the God whom Christians call 'father'? If you went round your local church and asked people that, you would (I suspect) get a wide variety of answers. Some will have been drawn in by the kindness and gentleness of a pastor, whether ordained or lay, who looked after them at a moment of crisis. Some will have gone to a meeting where they were able to express all kinds of questions and doubts and where they were received with courtesy and respect, and given such answers as were available – but it will be the courtesy and the respect that has done the trick. Others again may have found themselves at a major turning point in their lives and, not knowing where else to go for guidance, may have come to the church and found more than they expected.

This short but powerful song gives a quite different sort of reason why not only individuals but nations will come and worship the true and living God: 'your judgments have been revealed'. Since Revelation doesn't often talk about all the nations coming to worship (though ancient Jewish traditions about such things were well known, and the early Christians picked up on them to explain the arrival of so many non-Jews within the people of the Messiah), when it does it is worth pondering closely what it means. What are the 'judgments' of God? How have they been 'revealed'? And how has this brought the nations to worship?

When the Bible speaks about God 'judging', or putting into effect his 'judgments', it is just as much a cause for celebration as for anxiety. Think of the famous passages at the end of Psalms 96 and 98, where the whole of creation, animal and vegetable as well as human, sings for joy because YHWH is coming 'to judge the earth'. Why? Why is that good news?

Imagine a village in the outlying countryside of Judaea. It's a long way from the city, and even traders don't come there that often, far less government officials. A circuit judge comes to the neighbouring small town once every few months if they're lucky. But that doesn't mean that nothing needs doing. A builder is cheated by a customer, who refuses to admit his fault. A widow has her small purse stolen, and since she has nobody to plead for her she can do nothing. A family is evicted from their home by a landlord who thinks he can get more rent from someone else. And a fraudster with his eye on the main chance has accused a work colleague of cheating him, and though nothing has been done about it the other colleagues seem inclined to believe the charge. And so on. Nobody can do anything about any of these – until the judge comes.

When he comes, expectations will be massive. Months of pent-up frustrations will boil over. The judge will have to keep order, to calm down accusation and defence alike. He will have to hear each case properly and fairly, taking especial care for those with nobody to speak up for them. He will steadfastly refuse all bribes. And then he will *decide*. Judgment will be done. Chaos will be averted and order will be restored. The cheats will be put in their place, the thief punished and made to restore the purse. The grasping landlord will have to give way, and the false accuser will suffer the punishment he hoped to inflict. And the village as a whole will heave a sigh of relief. Justice has been done. The world has returned into balance. A grateful community will thank the judge from the bottom of its collective heart.

Now magnify the village concerns up to the global level. The wicked empire, and its local henchmen, have become more and more powerful, taking money, lives and pleasure as and when they please. It's no use appealing to the authorities, because it's the authorities who are doing the wrong. So the cry goes up to God, as it did to the God of Israel when the Egyptians were making their lives more and more miserable. And God's action on behalf of Israel is therefore a great act of liberating, healing, sigh-of-relief *judgment*. Things are put right at last.

We would expect, of course, that Israel itself would thank God for his rescue operation, his great act of 'judgment' which has set his people free. But the story of the Exodus, which is once again dominating John's horizon, goes further than that. It isn't only Israel that will see what God has done and give him thanks. The nations will look on and say to themselves, 'There really is a God in Israel; there really is a God who puts things right, who judges the earth' (see Psalm 58.11). And, saying that, they will come to worship him.

QUESTIONS FOR DISCUSSION AND REFLECTION

1 THE TEACHING OF JESUS

Prayer in secret (Matthew 6.5–6)
What are the key elements in the framework for prayer that Jesus provides?

The Lord's Prayer (Matthew 6.7–15)
What do the first section and second section of the Lord's Prayer focus on?

Ask, search, knock (Matthew 7.7–12)
Do you find it hard or easy to bring your everyday requests to God?

Persistence in prayer (Luke 11.1–13)
What does this passage teach about the character of God?

2 THE TEACHING OF PAUL

The Searcher of Hearts (Romans 8.22–23, 26–27)
What do you think Paul means by calling God the 'Searcher of Hearts'?

Praying with mind as well as spirit (1 Corinthians 14.13–19)
What does Paul consider important in the worshipping life of the church?

Practical prayer (Ephesians 6.18–20)

In what ways might prayer help you to fight spiritual battles?

Prayer for the world (1 Timothy 2.1–7)

When and why might you pray for those in positions of power and authority?

3 OTHER EARLY CHRISTIAN TEACHING

The sympathetic high priest (Hebrews 4.14–16)

How does it feel, and how does it affect the way you pray, knowing that Jesus sympathizes with your weaknesses?

Praying in faith (James 5.13–18)

In what ways do you think you could grow as a person who prays in faith?

4 PRAYERS OF JESUS

In the presence of God (Matthew 11.25–30)

What burdens are you carrying that you would like to bring to Jesus?

Glorify the son (John 17.1–8)

What is Jesus celebrating and what is he requesting in this prayer? How are the two connected?

Jesus prays for his people (John 17.9–19)

How might you use this prayer for yourself and for those you care about?

That they may be one (John 17.20–26)

In what ways could you or your community reach out to other kinds of Christians and express your desire to be at one with them?

Gethsemane (Matthew 26.36–46)

This is the second passage in Matthew's gospel where we see Jesus locked in a spiritual battle. How does this battle compare with the first one (in chapter 4)?

5 PRAYERS OF PAUL

To God be the glory (Romans 11.33–36)

How would you describe Paul's response to God's grace and covenant faithfulness, as expressed in this prayer?

To the only wise God (Romans 16.25–27)

In what sense is God, as revealed in Jesus, 'the only wise God'?

Grace, love and fellowship (2 Corinthians 13.13)

How does this prayer sum up what the Christian life is all about?

Blessings on the sovereign God! (Ephesians 1.3–10)

What blessings have you received in Jesus?

The inheritance and the spirit (Ephesians 1.11–14)

How does knowing you are to receive God's inheritance make a difference to the way you pray and live?

Knowing the power of the King (Ephesians 1.16–19)

How and why does Paul combine praise and petition in this prayer?

God's love, God's power – in us (Ephesians 3.14–21)

What are the characteristics of someone in whom God's love and power dwell?

Thanks, joy and overflowing love (Philippians 1.1–11)

Of whom can you say, 'I thank my God every time I think of you'?

Wisdom and gratitude (Colossians 1.9–14)

How might it help if someone were to pray this prayer for you?

Words of blessing (1 Thessalonians 3.11–13)

How does Paul's prayer reflect his desire for the church?

6 OTHER EARLY CHRISTIAN PRAYERS

Mary's song of praise (Luke 1.39–55)

In the spirit of Mary's song, what wrongs and injustices do you long to be put right in the world today?

Look upon their threats (Acts 4.23–31)

Is there something that is opposing your witness or your church's witness to Christ and, if so, how might your prayers make a difference?

The God of peace (Hebrews 13.20–21)

Is there anyone in particular for whom you would like to invoke the blessings of this prayer?

To the one and only God (Judah 24–25)

Can you think of ways in which God has kept you steady and 'unstumbling' in answer to prayer?

Praise to the creator (Revelation 4.6b–11)

What would you say are some of the most important reasons for worshipping and praising God?

Worthy is the lamb! (Revelation 5.8–14)

In the spirit of these two songs, how might you become more active in working as well as praying for God's coming kingdom?

The song of the lamb (Revelation 15.1–4)

What does it mean to pray for God's judgment to be revealed? And how can this be a cause for celebration?